COMPLETE HYPNOTISM, MESMERISM, MIND-READING AND SPIRITUALISM HOW TO HYPNOTIZE • ALPHEUS, A.

INTRODUCTION 1
--History of hypnotism--Mesmer--Puysegur--Braid--What is hypnotism?--Theories of hypnotism: 1. Animal magnetism; 2. The Neurosis Theory; 3. Suggestion Theory

CHAPTER I 7
--How to Hypnotize--Dr. Cocke's method-Dr. Flint's method--The French method at Paris--At Nancy--The Hindoo silent method--How to wake a subject from hypnotic sleep--Frauds of public hypnotic entertainments.

CHAPTER II 9
--Amusing experiments--Hypnotizing on the stage--"You can't pull your hands apart!"--Post-hypnotic suggestion--The newsboy, the hunter, and the young man with the rag doll--A whip becomes hot iron--Courting a broom stick--The side-show

CHAPTER III 11
--The stages of hypnotism--Lethargy-Catalepsy--The somnambulistic stage--Fascination

CHAPTER IV 15
--How the subject feels under hypnotization--Dr. Cocke's experience--Effect of music--Dr. Alfred Warthin's experiments

CHAPTER V 16
--Self hypnotization--How it may be done--An experience--Accountable for children's crusade--Oriental prophets self- hypnotized

CHAPTER VI 17
--Simulation--Deception in hypnotism very common--Examples of Neuropathic deceit--Detecting simulation--Professional subjects--How Dr. Luys of the Charity Hospital at Paris was deceived--Impossibility of detecting deception in all cases--Confessions of a professional hypnotic subject

CHAPTER VII.................. 20
--Criminal suggestion--Laboratory crimes--Dr. Cocke's experiments showing criminal suggestion is not possible--Dr. William James' theory--A bad man cannot be made good, why expect to make a good man bad?

CHAPTER VIII 22
--Dangers in being hypnotized Condemnation of public performances--A commonsense view--Evidence furnished by Lafontaine; by Dr. Courmelles; by Dr. Hart; by Dr. Cocke--No danger in hypnotism if rightly used by physicians or scientists

CHAPTER IX 24
--Hypnotism in medicine--Anesthesia--Restoring the use of muscles--Hallucination--Bad habits

CHAPTER X 26
--Hypnotism of animals--Snake charming

CHAPTER XI 27
--A scientific explanation of hypnotism--Dr. Hart's theory

CHAPTER XII............... 29
--Telepathy and Clairvoyance--Peculiar power in hypnotic state--Experiments--"Phantasms of the living" explained by telepathy

CHAPTER XIII 31

Publisher's Note

Purchase of this book entitles you to a free trial membership in the publisher's book club at www.rarebooksclub.com. (Time limited offer.) Simply enter the barcode number from the back cover onto the membership form on our home page. The book club entitles you to select from millions of books at no additional charge. You can also download a digital copy of this and related books to read on the go. Simply enter the title or subject onto the search form to find them.

Note: This is an historic book. Pages numbers, where present in the text, refer to the first edition of the book and may also be in indexes.

If you have any questions, could you please be so kind as to consult our Frequently Asked Questions page at www.rarebooksclub.com/faqs.cfm? You are also welcome to contact us there.
Publisher: General Books LLC™, Memphis, TN, USA, 2012. ISBN: 9781153596701.
Proofreading: pgdp.net

❧ ❧ ❧ ❧ ❧ ❧ ❧ ❧

**prepared by Jerry Kuntz
as part of the Lawson's Progress Project**

Complete Hypnotism: Mesmerism, Mind-Reading and Spiritualism

How to Hypnotize:
Being an Exhaustive and Practical System
of Method, Application, and Use

by A. Alpheus

1903

--The Confessions of a Medium--Spiritualistic phenomena explained on theory of telepathy--Interesting statement of Mrs. Piper, the famous medium of the Psychical Research Society
INTRODUCTION.

There is no doubt that hypnotism is a very old subject, though the name was not invented till 1850. In it was wrapped up the "mysteries of Isis" in Egypt thousands of years ago, and probably it was one of the weapons, if not the chief instrument of operation, of the magi mentioned in the Bible and of the "wise men" of Babylon and Egypt. "Laying on of hands" must have been a form of mesmerism, and Greek oracles of Delphi and other places seem to have been delivered by priests or priestesses who went into trances of self-induced hypnotism. It is suspected that the fakirs of

India who make trees grow from dry twigs in a few minutes, or transform a rod into a serpent (as Aaron did in Bible history), operate by some form of hypnotism. The people of the East are much more subject to influences of this kind than Western peoples are, and there can be no question that the religious orgies of heathendom were merely a form of that hysteria which is so closely related to the modern phenomenon of hypnotism. Though various scientific men spoke of magnetism, and understood that there was a power of a peculiar kind which one man could exercise over another, it was not until Frederick Anton Mesmer (a doctor of Vienna) appeared in 1775 that the general public gave any special attention to the subject. In the year mentioned, Mesmer sent out a circular letter to various scientific societies or "Academies" as they are called in Europe, stating his belief that "animal magnetism" existed, and that through it one man could influence another. No attention was given his letter, except by the Academy of Berlin, which sent him an unfavorable reply.

In 1778 Mesmer was obliged for some unknown reason to leave Vienna, and went to Paris, where he was fortunate in converting to his ideas d'Eslon, the Comte d'Artois's physician, and one of the medical professors at the Faculty of Medicine. His success was very great; everybody was anxious to be magnetized, and the lucky Viennese doctor was soon obliged to call in assistants. Deleuze, the librarian at the Jardin des Plantes, who has been called the Hippocrates of magnetism, has left the following account of Mesmer's experiments:

"In the middle of a large room stood an oak tub, four or five feet in diameter and one foot deep. It was closed by a lid made in two pieces, and encased in another tub or bucket. At the bottom of the tub a number of bottles were laid in convergent rows, so that the neck of each bottle turned towards the centre. Other bottles filled with magnetized water tightly corked up were laid in divergent rows with their necks turned outwards. Several rows were thus piled up, and the apparatus was then pronounced to be at 'high pressure'. The tub was filled with water, to which were sometimes added powdered glass and iron filings. There were also some dry tubs, that is, prepared in the same manner, but without any additional water. The lid was perforated to admit of the passage of movable bent rods, which could be applied to the different parts of the patient's body. A long rope was also fastened to a ring in the lid, and this the patients placed loosely round their limbs. No disease offensive to the sight was treated, such as sores, or deformities.

"A large number of patients were commonly treated at one time. They drew near to each other, touching hands, arms, knees, or feet. The handsomest, youngest, and most robust magnetizers held also an iron rod with which they touched the dilatory or stubborn patients. The rods and ropes had all undergone a 'preparation' and in a very short space of time the patients felt the magnetic influence. The women, being the most easily affected, were almost at once seized with fits of yawning and stretching; their eyes closed, their legs gave way and they seemed to suffocate. In vain did musical glasses and harmonicas resound, the piano and voices re-echo; these supposed aids only seemed to increase the patients' convulsive movements. Sardonic laughter, piteous moans and torrents of tears burst forth on all sides. The bodies were thrown back in spasmodic jerks, the respirations sounded like death rattles, the most terrifying symptoms were exhibited. Then suddenly the actors of this strange scene would frantically or rapturously rush towards each other, either rejoicing and embracing or thrusting away their neighbors with every appearance of horror.

"Another room was padded and presented another spectacle. There women beat their heads against wadded walls or rolled on the cushion-covered floor, in fits of suffocation. In the midst of this panting, quivering throng, Mesmer, dressed in a lilac coat, moved about, extending a magic wand toward the least suffering, halting in front of the most violently excited and gazing steadily into their eyes, while he held both their hands in his, bringing the middle fingers in immediate contact to establish communication. At another moment he would, by a motion of open hands and extended fingers, operate with the great current, crossing and uncrossing his arms with wonderful rapidity to make the final passes."

Hysterical women and nervous young boys, many of them from the highest ranks of Society, flocked around this wonderful wizard, and incidentally he made a great deal of money. There is little doubt that he started out as a genuine and sincere student of the scientific character of the new power he had indeed discovered; there is also no doubt that he ultimately became little more than a charlatan. There was, of course, no virtue in his "prepared" rods, nor in his magnetic tubs. At the same time the belief of the people that there was virtue in them was one of the chief means by which he was able to induce hypnotism, as we shall see later. Faith, imagination, and willingness to be hypnotized on the part of the subject are all indispensable to entire success in the practice of this strange art.

In 1779 Mesmer published a pamphlet entitled "Memoire sur la decouverte du magnetisme animal", of which Doctor Cocke gives the following summary (his chief claim was that he had discovered a principle which would cure every disease):

"He sets forth his conclusions in twenty-seven propositions, of which the substance is as follows:-- There is a reciprocal action and reaction between the planets, the earth and animate nature by means of a constant universal fluid, subject to mechanical laws yet unknown. The animal body is directly affected by the insinuation of this agent into the substance of the nerves. It causes in human bodies properties analogous to those of the magnet, for which reason it is called 'Animal Magnetism'. This magnetism may be communicated to other bodies, may be increased and reflected by mirrors, communicated, propagated, and accumulated, by sound. It may be accumulated, concentrated, and transported. The same rules apply to the opposite virtue. The magnet is susceptible of magnetism and the opposite virtue. The magnet and artificial electricity have, with respect to disease, properties common to a host of other agents presented to us by nature, and if the use of these has been attended by useful results, they are due to animal magnetism. By the aid of magnetism, then, the physician enlightened as to the use of medicine may render its action more perfect, and can provoke and direct salutary crises so as to have them completely under his control."

The Faculty of Medicine investigated Mesmer's claims, but reported unfavorably, and threatened d'Eslon with expulsion from the society unless he gave Mesmer up. Nevertheless the government favored the discoverer, and when the medical fraternity attacked him with such vigor that he felt obliged to leave Paris, it offered him a pension of 20,000 francs if he would remain. He went away, but later came back at the request of his pupils. In 1784 the government appointed two commissions to investigate the claims that had been made. On one of these commissions was Benjamin Franklin, then American Ambassador to France as well as the great French scientist Lavoisier. The other was drawn from the Royal Academy of Medicine, and included Laurent de Jussieu, the only man who declared in favor of Mesmer.

There is no doubt that Mesmer had returned to Paris for the purpose of making money, and these commissions were promoted in part by persons desirous of driving him out. "It is interesting," says a French writer, "to peruse the reports of these commissions: they read like a debate on some obscure subject of which the future has partly revealed the secret." Says another French writer (Courmelles): "They sought the fluid, not by the study of the cures affected, which was considered too complicated a task, but in the phases of mesmeric sleep. These were considered indispensable and easily regulated by the experimentalist. When submitted to close investigation, it was, however, found that they could only be induced when the subjects knew they were being magnetized, and that they differed according as they were conducted in public or in private. In short--whether it be a coincidence or the truth--imagination was considered the sole active agent. Whereupon d'Eslon remarked, 'If imagination is the best cure, why should we not use the imagination as a curative means?' Did he, who had so vaunted the existence of the fluid, mean by this to deny its existence, or was it rather a satirical way of saying. 'You choose to call it imagination; be it so. But after all, as it cures, let us make the most of it'?

"The two commissions came to the conclusion that the phenomena were due to imitation, and contact, that they were dangerous and must be prohibited. Strange to relate, seventy years later, Arago pronounced the same verdict!"

Daurent Jussieu was the only one who believed in anything more than this. He saw a new and important truth, which he set forth in a personal report upon withdrawing from the commission, which showed itself so hostile to Mesmer and his pretensions.

Time and scientific progress have largely overthrown Mesmer's theories of the fluid; yet Mesmer had made a discovery that was in the course of a hundred years to develop into an important scientific study. Says Vincent: "It seems ever the habit of the shallow scientist to plume himself on the more accurate theories which have been provided f, by the progress of knowledge and of science, and then, having been fed with a limited historical pabulum, to turn and talk lightly, and with an air of the most superior condescension, of the weakness and follies of those but for whose patient labors our modern theories would probably be non- existent." If it had not been for Mesmer and his "Animal Magnetism", we would never have had "hypnotism" and all our learned societies for the study of it.

Mesmer, though his pretensions were discredited, was quickly followed by Puysegur, who drew all the world to Buzancy, near Soissons, France. "Doctor Cloquet related that he saw there, patients no longer the victims of hysterical fits, but enjoying a calm, peaceful, restorative slumber. It may be said that from this moment really efficacious and useful magnetism became known." Every one rushed once more to be magnetized, and Puysegur had so many patients that to care for them all he was obliged to magnetize a tree (as he said), which was touched by hundreds who came to be cured, and was long known as "Puysegur's tree". As a result of Puysegur's success, a number of societies were formed in France for the study of the new phenomena.

In the meantime, the subject had attracted considerable interest in Germany, and in 1812 Wolfart was sent to Mesmer at Frauenfeld by the Prussian government to investigate Mesmerism. He became an enthusiast, and introduced its practice into the hospital at Berlin.

In 1814 Deleuze published a book on the subject, and Abbe Faria, who had come from India, demonstrated that there was no fluid, but that the phenomena were subjective, or within the mind of the patient. He first introduced what is now called the "method of suggestion" in producing magnetism or hypnotism. In 1815 Mesmer died.

Experimentation continued, and in the 20's Foissac persuaded the Academy of Medicine to appoint a commission to investigate the subject. After five years they presented a report. This report gave a good statement of the practical operation of magnetism, mentioning the phenomena of somnambulism, anesthesia, loss of memory, and the various other symptoms of the hypnotic state as we know it. It was thought that magnetism had a right to be considered as a therapeutic agent, and that it might be used by physicians, though others should not be allowed to practice it. In 1837 another commission made a decidedly unfavorable report.

Soon after this Burdin, a member of the Academy, offered a prize of 3,000 francs to any one who would read the number of a bank-note or the like with his eyes bandaged (under certain fixed conditions), but it was never awarded, though many claimed it, and there has been considerable evidence that persons in the hypnotic state have (sometimes) remarkable clairvoyant powers.

Soon after this, magnetism fell into very low repute throughout France and Germany, and scientific men became loath to have their names connected with the study of it in any way. The study had not yet been seriously taken up in England, and two physicians who gave some attention to it suffered decidedly in professional reputation.

It is to an English physician, however, that we owe the scientific character of modern hypnotism. Indeed he invented the name of hypnotism, formed from the Greek word meaning 'sleep', and designating 'artificially produced sleep'. His name is James Braid, and so important were the results of his study that hypnotism has sometimes been called "Braidism". Doctor Courmelles gives the following interesting summary of Braid's experiences:

"November, 1841, he witnessed a public experiment made by Monsieur Lafontaine, a Swiss magnetizer. He thought the whole thing a comedy; a week after, he attended a second exhibition, saw that the patient could not open his eyes, and concluded that this was ascribable to some physical cause. The fixity of gaze must, according to him, exhaust the nerve centers of the eyes and their surroundings. He made a friend look steadily at the neck of a bottle, and his own wife look at an ornamentation on the top of a china sugar bowl: sleep was the consequence. Here hypnotism had its origin, and the fact was established that sleep could be induced by physical agents. This, it must be remembered, is the essential difference between these two classes of phenomena (magnetism and hypnotism): for magnetism supposes a direct action of the magnetizer on the magnetized subject, an action which does not exist in hypnotism."

It may be stated that most English and American operators fail to see any distinction between magnetism and hypnotism, and suppose that the effect of passes, etc., as used by Mesmer, is in its way as much physical as the method of producing hypnotism by concentrating the gaze of the subject on a bright object, or the like.

Braid had discovered a new science--as far as the theoretical view of it was concerned--for he showed that hypnotism is largely, if not purely, mechanical and physical. He noted that during one phase of hypnotism, known as catalepsy, the arms, limbs, etc., might be placed in any position and would remain there; he also noted that a puff of breath would usually awaken a subject, and that by talking to a subject and telling him to do this or do that, even after he awakes from the sleep, he can be made to do those things. Braid thought he might affect a certain part of the brain during hypnotic sleep, and if he could find the seat of the thieving disposition, or the like, he could cure the patient of desire to commit crime, simply by suggestion, or command.

Braid's conclusions were, in brief, that there was no fluid, or other exterior agent, but that hypnotism was due to a physiological condition of the nerves. It was his belief that hypnotic sleep was brought about by fatigue of the eyelids, or by other influences wholly within the subject. In this he was supported by Carpenter, the great physiologist; but neither Braid nor Carpenter could get the medical organizations to give the matter any attention, even to investigate it. In 1848 an American named Grimes succeeded in obtaining all the phenomena of hypnotism, and created a school of writers who made use of the word "electro-biology."

In 1850 Braid's ideas were introduced into France, and Dr. Azam, of Bordeaux, published an account of them in the "Archives de Medicine." From this time on the subject was widely studied by scientific men in France and Germany, and it was more slowly taken up in England. It may be stated here that the French and other Latin races are much more easily hypnotized than the northern races, Americans perhaps being least subject to the hypnotic influence, and next to them the English. On the other hand, the Orientals are influenced to a degree we can hardly comprehend.

WHAT IS HYPNOTISM?

We have seen that so far the history of hypnotism has given us two manifestations, or methods, that of passes and playing upon the imagination in various ways, used by Mesmer, and that of physical means, such as looking at a bright object, used by Braid. Both of these methods are still in use, and though hundreds of scientific men, including many physicians, have studied the subject for years, no essentially new principle has been discovered, though the details of hypnotic operation have been thoroughly classified and many minor elements of interest have been developed. All these make a body of evidence which will assist us in answering the question, What is hypnotism?

Modern scientific study has pretty conclusively established the following facts:

1. Idiots, babies under three years old, and hopelessly insane people cannot be hypnotized.

2. No one can be hypnotized unless the operator can make him concentrate his attention for a reasonable length of time. Concentration of attention, whatever the method of producing hypnotism, is absolutely necessary.

3. The persons not easily hypnotized are those said to be neurotic (or those affected with hysteria). By "hysteria" is not meant nervous excitability, necessarily. Some very phlegmatic persons may be affected with hysteria. In medical science "hysteria" is an irregular action of the nervous system. It will sometimes show itself by severe pains in the arm, when in reality there is nothing whatever to cause pain; or it will raise a swelling on the head quite without cause. It is a tendency to nervous disease which in severe cases may lead to insanity. The word neurotic is a general term covering affection of the nervous system. It includes hysteria and much else beside.

On all these points practically every student of hypnotism is agreed. On the question as to whether any one can produce hypnotism by pursuing the right methods there is some disagreement, but not much. Dr. Ernest Hart in an article in the British Medical Journal makes the following very definite statement, representing the side of the case that maintains that any one can produce hypnotism. Says he:

"It is a common delusion that the mesmerist or hypnotizer counts for anything in the experiment. The operator, whether priest, physician, charlatan, self-deluded enthusiast, or conscious imposter, is not the source of any occult influence, does not possess any mysterious power, and plays only a very secondary and insignificant part in the chain of phenomena observed. There exist at the present time many individuals who claim for themselves, and some who make a living by so doing, a peculiar property or power as potent mesmerizers, hypnotizers, magnetizers, or electro-biologists. One even often hears it said in society (for I am sorry to say that these mischievous practices and pranks are sometimes made a society game) that such a person is a clever hypnotist or has great mesmeric or healing power. I hope to be able to prove, what I firmly hold, both from my own personal experience and experiment, as I have already related in the Nineteenth Century, that there is no such thing as a potent mesmeric influence, no such power resident in any one person more than another; that a glass of water, a tree, a stick, a penny-post letter, or a lime-light can mesmerize as effectually as can any individual. A clever hypnotizer means only a person who is acquainted with the physical or mental tricks by which the hypnotic condition is produced; or sometimes an unconscious imposter who is unaware of the very trifling part for which he is cast in the play, and who supposes himself really to possess a mysterious power which in, fact he does not possess at all, or which, to speak more accurately, is equally possessed by every stock or stone."

Against this we may place the statement of Dr. Foveau de Courmelles, who speaks authoritatively for the whole modern French school. He says:

"Every magnetizer is aware that certain individuals never can induce sleep even in the most easily hypnotizable subjects. They admit that the sympathetic fluid is necessary, and that each person may eventually find his or her hypnotizer, even when numerous attempts at inducing sleep have failed. However this may be, the impossibility some individuals find in inducing sleep in trained subjects, proves at least the existence of a negative force."

If you would ask the present writer's opinion, gathered from all the evidence before him, he would say that while he has no belief in the existence of any magnetic fluid, or anything that corresponds to it, he thinks there can be no doubt that some people will succeed as hypnotists while some will fail, just as some fail as carpenters while others succeed. This is true in every walk of life. It is also true that some people attract, others repel, the people they meet. This is not very easily explained, but we have all had opportunity to observe it. Again, since concentration is the prerequisite for producing hypnotism, one who has not the power of concentration himself, and concentration which he can perfectly control, is not likely to be able to secure it in others. Also, since faith is a strong element, a person who has not perfect self-confidence could not expect to create confidence in others. While many successful hypnotizers can themselves be hypnotized, it is probable that most all who have power of this kind are themselves exempt from the exercise of it. It is certainly true that while a person easily hypnotized is by no means weak-minded (indeed, it is probable that most geniuses would be good hypnotic subjects), still such persons have not a well balanced constitution and their nerves are high-strung if not unbalanced. They would be most likely to be subject to a person who had such a strong and well-balanced nervous constitution that it would be hard to hypnotize. And it is always safe to say that the strong may control the weak, but it is not likely that the weak will control the strong.

There is also another thing that must be taken into account. Science teaches that all matter is in vibration. Indeed, philosophy points to the theory that matter itself is nothing more than centers of force in vibration. The lowest vibration we know is that of sound. Then comes, at an enormously higher rate, heat, light (beginning at dark red and passing through the prismatic colors to violet which has a high vibration), to the chemical rays, and then the so-called X or unknown rays which have a much higher vibration still. Electricity is a form of vibration, and according to the belief of many scientists, life is a species of vibration so high that we have no possible means of measuring it. As every student of science knows, air appears to be the chief medium for conveying vibration of sound, metal is the chief medium for conveying electric vibrations, while to account for the vibrations of heat and light we have to assume (or imagine) an invisible, imponderable ether which fills all space and has no property of matter that we can distinguish except that of conveying vibrations of light in its various forms. When we pass on to human life, we have to theorize chiefly by analogy. (It must not be forgotten, however, that the existence of the ether and many assumed facts in science are only theories which have come to be generally adopted because they explain phenomena of all kinds better than any other theories which have been offered.)

Now, in life, as in physical science, any one who can get, or has by nature, the key-note of another nature, has a tremendous power over that other nature. The following story illustrates what this power is in the physical world. While we cannot vouch for the exact truth of the details of the story, there can be no doubt of the accuracy of the principle on which it is based:

"A musical genius came to the Suspension Bridge at Niagara Falls, and asked permission to cross; but as he had no money, his request was contemptuously refused. He stepped away from the entrance, and, drawing his violin from his case, began sounding notes up and down the scale. He finally discovered, by the thrill that sent a tremor through the mighty structure, that he had found the note on which the great cable that upheld the mass, was keyed. He drew his bow across the string of the violin again, and the colossal wire, as if under the spell of a magician, responded with a throb that sent a wave through its enormous length. He sounded the note again and again, and the cable that was dormant under the strain of loaded teams and monster engines-- the cable that remained stolid under the pressure of human traffic, and the heavy tread of commerce, thrilled and surged and shook itself, as mad waves of vibration coursed over its length, and it tore at its slack, until like a foam-crested wave of the sea, it shook the towers at either end, or, like some sentient animal, it tugged at its fetters and longed to be free.

"The officers in charge, apprehensive of danger, hurried the poor musician across, and bade him begone and trouble them no more. The ragged genius, putting his well-worn instrument back in its case, muttered to himself, 'I'd either crossed free or torn down the bridge.'"

"So the hypnotist," goes on the writer from which the above is quoted, "finds the note on which the subjective side of the person is attuned, and by playing upon it awakens into activity emotions and sensibilities that otherwise would have remained dormant, unused and even unsuspected."

No student of science will deny the truth of these statements. At the same time it has been demonstrated again and again that persons can and do frequently hypnotize themselves. This is what Mr. Hart means when he says that any stick or stone may produce hypnotism. If a person will gaze steadily at a bright fire, or a glass of water, for instance, he can throw himself into a hypnotic trance exactly similar to the condition produced by a professional or trained hypnotist. Such people, however, must be possessed of imagination.

THEORIES OF HYPNOTISM.

We have now learned some facts in regard to hypnotism; but they leave the subject still a mystery. Other facts which will be developed in the course of this book will only deepen the mystery. We will therefore state some of the best known theories.

Before doing so, however, it would be well to state concisely just what seems to happen in a case of hypnotism. The word hypnotism means sleep, and the definition of hypnotism implies artificially produced sleep. Sometimes this sleep is deep and lasting, and the patient is totally insensible; but the interesting phase of the condition is that in certain stages the patient is only partially asleep, while the other part of his brain is awake and very active.

It is well known that one part of the brain may be affected without affecting the other parts. In hemiplegia, for instance, one half of the nervous system is paralyzed, while the other half is all right. In the stages of hypnotism we will now consider, the will portion of the brain or mind seems to be put to sleep, while the other faculties are, abnormally awake. Some explain this by supposing that the blood is driven out of one portion of the brain and driven into other portions. In any case, it is as though the human engine were uncoupled, and the patient becomes an automaton. If he is told to do this, that, or the other, he does it, simply because his will is asleep and "suggestion", as it is called, from without makes him act just as he starts up unconsciously in his ordinary sleep if tickled with a straw.

Now for the theories. There are three leading theories, known as that of 1. Animal Magnetism; 2. Neurosis; and 3. Suggestion. We will simply state them briefly in order without discussion.

Animal Magnetism. This is the theory offered by Mesmer, and those who hold it assume that "the hypnotizer exercises a force, independently of suggestion, over the subject. They believe one part of the body to be charged separately, or that the whole body may be filled with magnetism. They recognize the power, of suggestion, but they do not believe it to be the principal factor in the production of the hypnotic state." Those who hold this theory today distinguish between the phenomena produced by magnetism and those produced by physical means or simple suggestion.

The Neurosis Theory. We have already explained the word neurosis, but we repeat here the definition given by Dr. J. R. Cocke. "A neurosis is any affection of the nervous centers occurring without any material agent producing it, without inflammation or any other constant structural change which can be detected in the nervous centers. As will be seen from the definition, any abnormal manifestation of the nervous system of whose cause we know practically nothing, is, for convenience, termed a neurosis. If a man has a certain habit or trick, it is termed a neurosis or neuropathic habit. One man of my acquaintance, who is a professor in a college, always begins his lecture by first sneezing and then pulling at his nose. Many forms of tremor are called neurosis. Now to say that hypnotism is the result of a. neurosis, simply means that a person's nervous system is susceptible to this condition, which, by M. Charcot and his followers, is regarded as abnormal." In short, M. Charcot places hypnotism in the same category of nervous affections in which hysteria and finally hallucination (medically considered) are to be classed, that is to say, as a nervous weakness, not to say a disease. According to this theory, a person whose nervous system is perfectly healthy could not be hypnotized. So many people can be hypnotized because nearly all the world is more or less insane, as a certain great writer has observed.

Suggestion. This theory is based on the power of mind over the body as we observe it in everyday life. Again let me quote from Dr. Cooke. "If we can direct the subject's whole attention to the belief that such an effect as before mentioned--that his arm will be paralyzed, for instance--will take place, that effect will gradually occur. Such a result having been once produced, the subject's will-power and power of resistance are considerably weakened, because he is much more inclined than at first to believe the hypnotizer's assertion. This is generally the first step in the process of hypnosis. The method pursued at the school of Nancy is to convince the subject that his eyes are closing by directing his attention to that effect as strongly as possible. However, it is not necessary that we begin with the eyes. According to M. Dessoir, any member of the body will answer as well." The theory of Suggestion is maintained by the medical school attached to the hospital at Nancy. The theory of Neurosis was originally put forth as the result of experiments by Dr. Charcot at the Salpetriere hospital in Paris, which is now the co-called Salpetriere school-- that is the medical, school connected with the Salpetriere hospital.

There is also another theory put forth, or rather a modification of Professor Charcot's theory, and maintained by the school of the Charity hospital in Paris, headed by Dr. Luys, to the effect that the physical magnet and electricity may affect persons in the hypnotic state, and that certain drugs in sealed tubes placed upon the patient's neck during the condition of hypnosis will produce the same effects which those drugs would produce if taken internally, or as the nature of the drugs would seem to call for if imbibed in a more complete fashion. This school, however, has been considerably discredited, and Dr. Luys' conclusions are not received by scientific students of hypnotism. It is also stated, and the present writer has seen no effective denial, that hypnotism may be produced by pressing with the fingers upon certain points in the body, known as hypnogenic spots.

It will be seen that these three theories stated above are greatly at variance with each other. The student of hypnotism will have to form a conclusion for himself as he investigates the facts. Possibly it will be found that the true theory is a combination of all three of those described above. Hypnotism is certainly a complicated phenomena, and he would be a rash man who should try to explain it in a sentence or in a paragraph. An entire book proves a very limited space for doing it.

CHAPTER I.
HOW TO HYPNOTIZE.

Dr. Cocke's Method--Dr. Flint's Method--The French Method at Paris-- at Nancy--The Hindoo Silent Method-- How to Wake a Subject from Hypnotic Sleep--Frauds of Public Hypnotic Entertainers.

First let us quote what is said of hypnotism in Foster's Encyclopedic Medical Dictionary. The dictionary states the derivation of the word from the Greek word meaning sleep, and gives as synonym "Braidism". This definition follows: "An abnormal state into which some persons may be thrown, either by a voluntary act of their own, such as gazing continuously with fixed attention on some bright object held close to the eyes, or by the exercise of another person's will; characterized by suspension of the will and consequent obedience to the promptings of suggestions from without. The activity of the organs of special sense, except the eye, may be heightened, and the power of the muscles increased. Complete insensibility to pain may be induced by hypnotism, and it has been used as an anaesthetic. It is apt to be followed by a severe headache of long continuance, and by various nervous disturbances. On emerging from the hypnotic state, the person hypnotized usually has no remembrance of what happened during its continuance, but in many persons such remembrance may be induced by 'suggestion'. About one person in three is susceptible to hypnotism, and those of the hysterical or neurotic tendency (but rarely the insane) are the most readily hypnotized."

First we will quote the directions for producing hypnotism given by Dr. James R. Cocke, one of the most scientific experimenters in hypnotism in America. His directions of are special value, since they are more applicable to American subjects than the directions given by French writers. Says Dr. Cocke:

"The hypnotic state can be produced in one of the following ways: First, command the subject to close his eyes. Tell him his mind is a blank. Command him to think of nothing. Leave him a few minutes; return and tell him he cannot open his eyes. If he fails to do so, then begin to make any suggestion which may be desired. This is the so-called mental method of hypnotization.

"Secondly, give the subject a coin or other bright object. Tell him to look steadfastly at it and not take his eyes away from it. Suggest that his eyelids are growing heavy, that he cannot keep them open. Now close the lids. They cannot be opened. This is the usual method employed by public exhibitors. A similar method is by looking into a mirror, or into a glass of water, or by rapidly revolving polished disks, which should be looked at steadfastly in the same way as is the coin, and I think tires the eyes less.

"Another method is by simply commanding the subject to close his eyes, while the operator makes passes over his head and hands without coming in contact with them. Suggestions may be made during these passes.

"Fascination, as it is called, is one of the hypnotic states. The operator fixes his eyes on those of the subject. Holding his attention for a few minutes, the operator begins to walk backward; the subject follows. The operator raises the arm; the subject does likewise. Briefly, the subject will imitate any movement of the hypnotist, or will obey any suggestion made by word, look or gesture, suggested by the one with whom he is en rapport.

"A very effective method of hypnotizing a person is by commanding him to sleep, and having some very soft music played upon the piano, or other stringed instrument. Firm pressure over the orbits, or over the finger- ends and root of the nail for some minutes may also induce the condition of hypnosis in very sensitive persons.

"Also hypnosis can frequently be induced by giving the subject a glass of water, and telling him at the same time that it has been magnetized. The wearing of belts around the body, and rings round the fingers, will also, sometimes, induce a degree of hypnosis, if the subject has been told that they have previously been magnetized or are electric.

The latter descriptions are the so-called physical methods described by Dr. Moll."

Dr. Herbert L. Flint, a stage hypnotizer, describes his methods as follows:

"To induce hypnotism, I begin by friendly conversation to place my patient in a condition of absolute calmness and quiescence. I also try to win his confidence by appealing to his own volitional effort to aid me in obtaining the desired clad. I impress upon him that hypnosis in his condition is a benign agency, and far from subjugating his mentality, it becomes intensified to so great an extent as to act as a remedial agent.

"Having assured myself that he is in a passive condition, I suggest to him, either with or without passes, that after looking intently at an object for a few moments, he will experience a feeling of lassitude. I steadily gaze at his eyes, and in a monotonous tone I continue to suggest the various stages of sleep. As for instance, I say, 'Your breathing is heavy. Your whole body is relaxed.' I raise his arm, holding it in a horizontal position for a second or two, and suggest to him that it is getting heavier and heavier. I let my hand go and his arm falls to his side.

"'Your eyes,' I continue, 'feel tired and sleepy. They are fast closing' repeating in a soothing tone the words 'sleepy, sleepy, sleep.' Then in a self-assertive tone, I emphasize the suggestion by saying in an unhesitating and positive tone, 'sleep.'

"I do not, however, use this method with all patients. It is an error to state, as some specialists do, that from their formula there can be no deviation; because, as no two minds are constituted alike, so they cannot be affected alike. While one will yield by intense will exerted through my eyes, another may, by the same means, become fretful, timid, nervous, and more wakeful than he was before. The same rule applies to gesture, tones of the voice, and mesmeric passes. That which has a soothing and lulling effect on one, may have an opposite effect on another. There can be no unvarying rule applicable to all patients. The means must be left to the judgment of the operator, who by a long course of psychological training should be able to judge what measures are necessary to obtain control of his subject. Just as in drugs, one person may take a dose without injury that will kill another, so in hypnosis, one person can be put into a deep sleep by means that would be totally ineffectual in another, and even then the mental states differ in each individual--that which in one induces a gentle slumber may plunge his neighbor into a deep cataleptic state."

That hypnotism may be produced by purely physical or mechanical means seems to have been demonstrated by an incident which started Doctor Burq, a Frenchman, upon a scientific inquiry which lasted many years. "While practising as a young doctor, he had one day been obliged to go out and had deemed it advisable to lock up a patient in his absence. Just as he was leaving the house he heard the sound as of a body suddenly falling. He hurried back into the room and found his patient in a state of catalepsy. Monsieur Burq was at that time studying magnetism, and he at once sought for the cause of this phenomenon. He noticed that the door-handle was of copper. The next day he wrapped a glove around the handle, again shut the patient in, and this time nothing occurred. He interrogated the patient, but she could give him no explanation. He then tried the effect of copper on all the subjects at the Salpetriere and the Cochin hospitals, and found that a great number were affected by it."

At the Charity hospital in Paris, Doctor Luys used an apparatus moved by clockwork. Doctor Foveau, one of his pupils, thus describes it:

"The hypnotic state, generally produced by the contemplation of a bright spot, a lamp, or the human eye, is in his case induced by a peculiar kind of mirror. The mirrors are made of pieces of wood cut prismatically in which fragments of mirrors are incrusted. They are generally double and placed crosswise, and by means of clockwork revolve automatically. They are the same as sportsmen use to attract larks, the rays of the sun being caught and reflected on every side and from all points of the horizon. If the little mirrors in each branch are placed in parallel lines in front of a patient, and the rotation is rapid, the optic organ soon becomes fatigued, and a calming soothing somnolence ensues. At first it is not a deep sleep, the eye-lids are scarcely heavy, the drowsiness slight and restorative. By degrees, by a species of training, the hypnotic sleep differs more and more from natural sleep, the individual abandons himself more and more completely, and falls into one of the regular phases of hypnotic sleep. Without a word, without a suggestion or any other action, Dr. Luys has made wonderful cures. Wecker, the occulist, has by the same means entirely cured spasms of the eye-lids."

Professor Delboeuf gives the following account of how the famous Liebault produced hypnotism at the hospital at Nancy. We would especially ask the reader to note what he says of Dr. Liebault's manner and general bearing, for without doubt much of his success was due to his own personality. Says Professor Delboeuf:

"His modus faciendi has something ingenious and simple about it, enhanced by a tone and air of profound conviction; and his voice has such fervor and warmth that he carries away his clients with him.

"After having inquired of the patient what he is suffering from, without any further or closer examination, he places his hand on the patient's forehead and, scarcely looking at him, says, 'You are going to sleep.' Then, almost immediately, he closes the eyelids, telling him that he is asleep. After that he raises the patient's arm, and says, 'You cannot put your arm down.' If he does, Dr. Liebault appears hardly to notice it. He then turns the patient's arm around, confidently affirming that the movement cannot be stopped, and saying this he turns his own arms rapidly around, the patient remaining all the time with his eyes shut; then the doctor talks on without ceasing in a loud and commanding voice. The suggestions begin:

"'You are going to be cured; your digestion will be good, your sleep quiet, your cough will stop, your circulation will become free and regular; you are going to feel very strong and well, you will be able to walk about,' etc., etc. He hardly ever varies the speech. Thus he fires away at every kind of disease at once, leaving it to the client to find out his own. No doubt he gives some special directions, according to the disease the patient is suffering from, but general instructions are the chief thing.

"The same suggestions are repeated a great many times to the same person, and, strange to say, notwithstanding the inevitable monotony of the speeches, and the uniformity of both style and voice, the master's tone is so ardent, so penetrating, so sympathetic, that I have never once listened to it without a feeling of intense admiration."

The Hindoos produce sleep simply by sitting on the ground and, fixing their eyes steadily on the subject, swaying the body in a sort of writhing motion above the hips. By continuing this steadily and in perfect silence for ten or fifteen minutes before a large audience, dozens can be put to sleep at one time. In all cases, freedom from noise or distractive incidents is essential to success in hypnotism, for concentration must be produced.

Certain French operators maintain that hypnotism may be produced by pressure on certain hypnogenic points or regions of the body. Among these are the eye-balls, the crown of the head, the back of the neck and the upper bones of the spine between the shoulder glades. Some persons may be hypnotized by gently pressing on the skin at the base of the finger-nails, and at the root of the nose; also by gently scratching the neck over the great nerve center.

Hypnotism is also produced by sudden noise, as if by a Chinese gong, etc.

HOW TO WAKE A SUBJECT FROM HYPNOTIC SLEEP.

This is comparatively easy in moot cases. Most persons will awake naturally at the end of a few minutes, or will fall into a natural sleep from which in an hour or two they will awake refreshed. Usually the operator simply says to the subject, "All right, wake up now," and claps his hands or makes some other decided noise. In some cases it is sufficient to say, "You will wake up in five minutes"; or tell a subject to count twelve and when he gets to ten say, "Wake up."

Persons in the lethargic state are not susceptible to verbal suggestions, but may be awakened by lifting both eyelids.

It is said that pressure on certain regions will wake the subject, just as pressure in certain other places will put the subject to sleep. Among these places for awakening are the ovarian regions.

Some writers recommend the application of cold water to awaken subjects, but this is rarely necessary. In olden times a burning coal was brought near.

If hypnotism was produced by passes, then wakening may be brought about by passes in the opposite direction, or with the back of the hand toward the subject.

The only danger is likely to be found in hysterical persons. They will, if aroused, often fall off again into a helpless state, and continue to do so for some time to come. It is dangerous to hypnotize such subjects.

Care should be taken to awaken the subject very thoroughly before leaving him, else headache, nausea, or the like may follow, with other unpleasant effects. In all cases subjects should be treated gently and with the utmost consideration, as if the subject and operator were the most intimate friends.

It is better that the person who induces hypnotic sleep should awaken the subject. Others cannot do it so easily, though as we have said, subjects usually awaken themselves after a short time.

Further description of the method of producing hypnotism need not be given; but it is proper to add that in addition to the fact that not more than one person out of three can be hypnotized at all, even by an experienced operator, to effect hypnotization except in a few cases requires a great deal of patience, both on the part of the operator and of the subject. It may require half a dozen or more trials before any effect at all can be produced, although in some cases the effect will come within a minute or two. After a person has been once hypnotized, hypnotization is much easier. The most startling results are to be obtained only after a long process of training on the part of the subject. Public hypnotic entertainments, and even those given at the hospitals in Paris, would be quite impossible if trained subjects were not at hand; and in the case of the public hypnotizer, the proper subjects are hired and placed in the audience for the express purpose of coming forward when called for. The success of such an entertainment could not otherwise be guaranteed. In many cases, also, this training of subjects makes them deceivers. They learn to imitate what they see, and since their living depends upon it, they must prove hypnotic subjects who can always be depended upon to do just what is wanted. We may add, however, that what they do is no more than an imitation of the real thing. There is no grotesque manifestation on the stage, even if it is a pure fake, which could not be matched by more startling facts taken from undoubted scientific experience.

CHAPTER II.

AMUSING EXPERIMENTS.

Hypnotizing on the Stage--"You Can't Pull Your Hands Apart"--Post Hypnotic Suggestion--The News boy, the Hunter, and the Young Man with the Rag Doll--A Whip Becomes Hot Iron--Courting a Broomstick--The Side Show.

Let us now describe some of the manifestations of hypnotism, to see just how it operates and how it exhibits itself. The following is a description of a public performance given by Dr. Herbert L. Flint, a very successful public operator. It is in the language of an eye-witness-- a New York lawyer.

In response to a call for volunteers, twenty young and middle-aged men came upon the stage. They evidently belonged to the great middle-class. The entertainment commenced by Dr. Flint passing around the group, who were seated on the stage in a semicircle facing the audience, and stroking each one's head and forehead, repeating the phrases, "Close your eyes. Think of nothing but sleep. You are very tired. You are drowsy. You feel very sleepy." As he did this, several of the volunteers closed their eyes at once, and one fell asleep immediately. One or two remained awake, and these did not give themselves up to the influence, but rather resisted it.

When the doctor had completed his round and had manipulated all the volunteers, some of those influenced were nodding, some were sound asleep, while a few were wide awake and smiling at the rest. These latter were dismissed as unlikely subjects.

When the stage had been cleared of all those who were not responsive, the doctor passed around, and, snapping his finger at each individual, awoke him. One of the subjects when questioned afterward as to what sensation he experienced at the snapping of the fingers, replied that it seemed to him as if something inside of his head responded, and with this sensation he regained self-consciousness. (This is to be doubted. As a rule, subjects in this stage of hypnotism do not feel any sensation that they can remember, and do not become self-conscious.)

The class was now apparently wide awake, and did not differ in appearance from their ordinary state. The doctor then took each one and subjected him to a separate physical test, such as sealing the eyes, fastening the hands, stiffening the fingers, arms, and legs, producing partial catalepsy and causing stuttering and inability to speak. In those possessing strong imaginations, he was able to produce hallucinations, such as feeling mosquito bites, suffering from toothache, finding the pockets filled and the hands covered with molasses, changing identity, and many similar tests.

The doctor now asked each one to clasp his hands in front of him, and when all had complied with the request, he repeated the phrase, "Think your hands so fast that you can't pull them apart. They are fast. You cannot pull them apart. Try. You can't." The whole class made frantic efforts to unclasp their hands, but were unable to do so. The doctor's explanation of this is, that what they were really doing was to force their hands closer together, thus obeying the counter suggestion. That they thought they were trying to unclasp their hands was evident from their endeavors.

The moment he made them desist, by snapping his fingers, the spell was broken. It was most astonishing to see that as each one awoke, he seemed to be fully cognizant of the ridiculous position in which his comrades were placed, and to enjoy their confusion and ludicrous attitudes. The moment, however, he was commanded to do things equally absurd, he obeyed. While, therefore, the class appeared to be free agents, they are under hypnotic control.

One young fellow, aged about eighteen, said that he was addicted to the cigarette habit. The suggestion was made to him that he would not be able to smoke a cigarette for twenty-four hours. After the entertainment he was asked to smoke, as was his usual habit. He was then away from any one who could influence him. He replied that the very idea was repugnant. However, he was induced to take a cigarette in his mouth, but it made him ill and he flung it away with every expression of disgust. *This is an instance of what is called post-hypnotic suggestion. Dr. Cocke tells of suggesting to a drinker whom he was trying to cure of the habit that for the next three days anything he took would make him vomit; the result followed as suggested.

The same phenomena that was shown in unclasping the hands, was next exhibited in commanding the subjects to rotate them. They immediately began and twirled them faster and faster, in spite of their efforts to stop. One of the subjects said he thought of nothing but the strange action of his hands, and sometimes it puzzled him to know why they whirled.

At this point Dr. Flint's daughter took charge of the class. She pointed her finger at one of them, and the subject began to look steadily before him, at which the rest of the class were highly amused. Presently the subject's head leaned forward, the pupils of his eyes dilated and assumed a peculiar glassy stare. He arose with a steady, gliding gait and walked up to the lady until his nose touched her hand. Then he stopped. Miss Flint led him to the front of the stage and left him standing in profound slumber. He stood there, stooping, eyes set, and vacant, fast asleep. In the meantime the act had caused great laughter among the rest of the class. One young fellow in particular, laughed so uproariously that tears coursed down his cheeks, and he took out his handkerchief to wipe his eyes. Just as he was returning it to his pocket, the lady suddenly pointed a finger at him. She was in the center of the stage, fully fifteen feet away from the subject, but the moment the gesture was made, his countenance fell, his mirth stopped, while that of his companions redoubled, and the change was so obvious that the audience shared in the laughter--but the subject neither saw nor heard. His eyes assumed the same expression that had been noticed in his companion's. He, too, arose in the same attitude, as if his head were pulling the body along, and following the finger in the same way as his predecessor, was conducted to the front of the stage by the side of the first subject. This was repeated on half a dozen subjects, and the manifestations were the same in each case. Those selected were now drawn up in an irregular line in front of the stage, their eyes fixed on vacancy, their heads bent forward, perfectly motionless. Each was then given a suggestion. One was to be a newsboy, and sell papers. Another was given a broomstick and told to hunt game in the woods before him. Another was given a large rag doll and told that it was an infant, and that he must look among the audience and discover the father. He was informed that he could tell who the father was by the similarity and the color of the eyes.

These suggestions were made in a loud tone, Miss Flint being no nearer one subject than another. The bare suggestion was given, as, "Now, think that you are a newsboy, and are selling papers," or, "Now think that you are hunting and are going into the woods to shoot birds."

So the party was started at the same time into the audience. The one who was impersonating a newsboy went about crying his edition in a loud voice; while the hunter crawled along stealthily and carefully. The newsboy even adopted the well-worn device of asking those whom he solicited to buy to help him get rid of his stock. One man offered him a cent, when the price was two cents. The newsboy chaffed the would-be purchaser. He sarcastically asked him if he "didn't want the earth."

The others did what they had been told to do in the same earnest, characteristic way.

After this performance, the class was again seated in a semicircle, and Miss Flint selected one of them, and, taking him into the center of the stage, showed him a small riding whip. He looked at it indifferently enough. He was told it was a hot bar of iron, but he shook his head, still incredulous. The suggestion was repeated, and as the glazed look came into his eyes, the incredulous look died out. Every member of the class was following the suggestion made to the subject in hand. All of them had the same expression in their eyes. The doctor said that his daughter was hypnotizing the whole class through this one individual.

As she spoke she lightly touched the subject with the end of the whip. The moment the subject felt the whip he jumped and shrieked as if it really were a hot iron. She touched each one of the class in succession, and every one manifested the utmost pain and fear. One subject sat down on the floor and cried in dire distress. Others, when touched, would tear off their clothing or roll up their sleeves. One young man was examined by a physician present just after the whip had been laid across his shoulders, and a long red mark was found, just such a one as would have been made by a real hot iron. The doctor said that, had the suggestion been continued, it would undoubtedly have raised a blister.

One of the amusing experiments tried at a later time was that of a tall young man, diffident, pale and modest, being given a broom carefully wrapped in a sheet, and told that it was his sweetheart. He accepted the situation and sat down by the broom. He was a little sheepish at first, but eventually he grew bolder, and smiled upon her such a smile as Malvolio casts upon Olivia. The manner in which, little by little, he ventured upon a familiar footing, was exceedingly funny; but when, in a moment of confident response to his wooing, he clasped her round the waist and imprinted a chaste kiss upon the brushy part of the broom, disguised by the sheet, the house resounded with roars of laughter. The subject, however, was deaf to all of the noise. He was absorbed in his courtship, and he continued to hug the broom, and exhibit in his features that idiotic smile that one sees only upon the faces of lovers and bridegrooms. "All the world loves a lover," as the saying is, and all the world loves to laugh at him.

One of the subjects was told that the head of a man in the audience was on fire. He looked for a moment, and then dashed down the platform into the audience, and, seizing the man's head, vigorously rubbed it. As this did not extinguish the flames, he took off his coat and put the fire out. In doing this, he set his coat on fire, when he trampled it under foot. Then he calmly resumed his garment and walked back to the stage.

The "side-show" closed the evening's entertainment. A young man was told to think of himself as managing a side-show at a circus. When his mind had absorbed this idea he was ordered to open his exhibition. He at once mounted a table, and, in the voice of the traditional side-show fakir, began to dilate upon the fat woman and the snakes, upon the wild man from Borneo, upon the learned pig, and all the other accessories of side-shows. He went over the usual characteristic "patter," getting more and more in earnest, assuring his hearers that for the small sum of ten cents they could see more wonders than ever before had been crowded under one canvas tent. He harangued the crowd as they surged about the tent door. He pointed to a suppositious canvas picture. He "chaffed" the boys. He flattered the vanity of the young fellows with their girls, telling them that they could not afford, for the small sum of ten cents, to miss this great show. He made change for his patrons. He indulged in side remarks, such as "This is hot work." He rolled up his sleeves and took off his collar and necktie, all of the time expatiating upon the merits of the freaks inside of his tent.

CHAPTER III.

THE STAGES OF HYPNOTISM.

Lethargy--Catalepsy--The Somnambulistic Stage--Fascination.

We have just given some of the amusing experiments that may be performed with subjects in one of the minor stages of hypnotism. But there are other stages which give entirely different manifestations. For a scientific classification of these we are indebted to Professor Charcot, of the Salpetriere hospital in Paris, to whom, next to Mesmer and Braid, we are indebted for the present science of hypnotism. He recognized three distinct stages--lethargy, catalepsy and somnambulism. There is also a condition of extreme lethargy, a sort of trance state, that lasts for days and even weeks, and, indeed, has been known to last for years. There is also a lighter phase than somnambulism, that is called fascination. Some doctors, however, place it between catalepsy and somnambulism. Each of these stages is marked by quite distinct phenomena. We give them as described by a pupil of Dr. Charcot.

LETHARGY.

This is a state of absolute inert sleep. If the method of Braid is used, and a bright object is held quite near the eyes, and the eyes are fixed upon it, the subject squints, the eyes become moist and bright, the look fixed, and the pupils dilated. This is the cataleptic stage. If the object is left before the eyes, lethargy is produced. There are also many other ways of producing lethargy, as we have seen in the chapter "How to Hypnotize.

"One of the marked characteristics of this stage of hypnotism is the tendency of the muscles to contract, under the influence of the slightest touch, friction, pressure or massage, or even that of a magnet placed at a distance. The contraction disappears only by the repetition of that identical means that called it into action. Dr. Courmelles gives the following illustration:

"If the forearm is rubbed a little above the palm of the hand, this latter yields and bends at an acute angle. The subject may be suspended by the hand, and the body will be held up without relaxation, that is, without returning to the normal condition. To return to the normal state, it suffices to rub the antagonistic muscles, or, in ordinary terms, the part diametrically opposed to that which produced the phenomenon; in this case, the forearm a little above the hands. It is the same for any other part of the body."

The subject appears to be in a deep sleep, the eyes are either closed or half closed, and the face is without expression. The body appears to be in a state of complete collapse, the head is thrown back, and the arms and legs hang loose, dropping heavily down. In this stage insensibility is so complete that needles can be run into any part of the body without producing pain, and surgical operations may be performed without the slightest unpleasant effect.

This stage lasts usually but a short time, and the patient, under ordinary conditions, will pass upward into the stage of catalepsy, in which he opens his eyes. If the hypnotism is spontaneous, that is, if it is due to a condition of the nervous organism which has produced it without any outside aid, we have the condition of prolonged trance, of which many cases have been reported. Until the discovery of hypnotism these strange trances were little understood, and people were even buried alive in them. A few instances reported by medical men will be interesting. There is one reported in 1889 by a noted French physician. Said he:

"There is at this moment in the hospital at Mulhouse a most interesting case. A young girl twenty-two years of age has been asleep here for the last twelve days. Her complexion is fresh and rosy, her breathing quite normal, and her features unaltered.

"No organ seems attacked; all the vital functions are performed as in the waking state. She is fed with milk, broth and wine, which is given her in a spoon. Her mouth even sometimes opens of itself at the contact of the spoon, and she swallows without the slightest difficulty. At other times the gullet remains inert.

"The whole body is insensible. The forehead alone presents, under the action of touch or of pricks, some reflex phenomena. However, by a peculiarity, which is extremely interesting, she seems, by the intense horror she shows for ether, to retain a certain amount of consciousness and sensibility. If a drop of ether is put into her mouth her face contracts and assumes an expression of disgust. At the same moment her arms and legs are violently agitated, with the kind of impatient motion that a child displays when made to swallow some hated dose of medicine.

"In the intellectual relations the brain is not absolutely obscure, for on her mother's coming to see her the subject's face became highly colored, and tears appeared on the tips of her eyelashes, without, however, in any other way disturbing her lethargy.

"Nothing has yet been able to rouse her from this torpor, which will, no doubt, naturally disappear at a given moment. She will then return to conscious life as she quitted it. It is probable that she will not retain any recollection of her present condition, that all notion of time will fail her, and that she will fancy it is only the day following her usual nightly slumber, a slumber which, in this case, has been transformed into a lethargic sleep, without any rigidity of limbs or convulsions.

"Physically, the sleeper is of a middle size, slender, strong and pretty, without distinctive characteristic. Mentally, she is lively, industrious, sometimes whimsical, and subject to slight nervous attacks."

There is a pretty well-authenticated report of a young girl who, on May 30, 1883, after an intense fright, fell into a lethargic condition which lasted for four years. Her parents were poor and ignorant, but, as the fame of the case spread abroad, some physicians went to investigate it in March, 1887. Her sleep had never been interrupted. On raising the eyelids, the doctors found the eyes turned convulsively upward, but, blowing upon them, produced no reflex movement of the lids. Her jaws were closed tightly, and the attempt to open her mouth had broken off some of the teeth level with the gums. The muscles contracted at the least breath or touch, and the arms remained in position when uplifted. The contraction of the muscles is a sign of the lethargic state, but the arm, remaining in position, indicates the cataleptic state. The girl was kept alive by liquid nourishment poured into her mouth.

There are on record a large number of cases of persons who have slept for several months.

CATALEPSY.

The next higher stage of hypnotism is that of catalepsy. Patients may be thrown into it directly, or patients in the lethargic state may be brought into it by lifting the eyelids. It seems that the light penetrating the eyes, and affecting the brain, awakens new powers, for the cataleptic state has phenomena quite peculiar to itself.

Nearly all the means for producing hypnotism will, if carried to just the right degree, produce catalepsy. For instance, besides the fixing of the eye on a bright object, catalepsy may be produced by a sudden sound, as of a Chinese gong, a tom-tom or a whistle, the vibration of a tuning-fork, or thunder. If a solar spectrum is suddenly brought into a dark room it may produce catalepsy, which is also produced by looking at the sun, or a lime light, or an electric light.

In this state the patient has become perfectly rigidly fixed in the position in which he happens to be when the effect is produced, whether sitting, standing, kneeling, or the like; and this face has an expression of fear. The arms or legs may be raised, but if left to themselves will not drop, as in lethargy. The eyes are wide open, but the look is fixed and impassive. The fixed position lasts only a few minutes, however, when the subject returns to a position of relaxation, or drops back into the lethargic state.

If the muscles, nerves or tendons are rubbed or pressed, paralysis may be produced, which, however, is quickly removed by the use of electricity, when the patient awakes. By manipulating the muscles the most rigid contraction may be produced, until the entire body is in such a state of corpse-like rigidity that a most startling experiment is possible. The subject may be placed with his head upon the back of one chair and his heels on the back of another, and a heavy man may sit upon him without seemingly producing any effect, or even heavy rock may be broken on the subject's body.

Messieurs Binet and Fere, pupils of the Salpetriere school, describe the action of magnets on cataleptic subjects, as follows:

"The patient is seated near a table, on which a magnet has been placed, the left elbow rests on the arm of the chair, the forearm and hand vertically upraised with thumb and index finger extended, while the other fingers remain half bent. On the right side the forearm and hand are stretched on the table, and the magnet is placed under a linen cloth at a distance of about two inches. After a couple of minutes the right index begins to tremble and rise up; on the left side the extended fingers bend down, and the hand remains limp for an instant. The right hand and forearm rise up and assume the primitive position of the left hand, which is now stretched out on the arm of the chair, with the waxen pliability that pertains to the cataleptic state."

An interesting experiment may be tried by throwing a patient into lethargy on one side and catalepsy on the other. To induce what is called hemi-lethargy and hemi-catalepsy is not difficult. First, the lethargic stage is induced, then one eyelid is raised, and that side alone becomes cataleptic, and may be operated on in various interesting ways. The arm on that side, for instance, will remain raised when lifted, while the arm on the other side will fall heavily.

Still more interesting is the intellectual condition of the subject. Some great man has remarked that if he wished to know what a person was thinking of, he assumed the exact position and expression of that person, and soon he would begin to feel and think just as the other was thinking and feeling. Look a part and you will soon begin to feel it.

In the cataleptic subject there is a close relation between the attitude the subject assumes and the intellectual manifestation. In the somnambulistic stage patients are manipulated by speaking to them; in the cataleptic stage they are equally under the will of the operator; but now he controls them by gesture. Says Dr. Courmelles, from his own observation: "The emotions in this stage are made at command, in the true acceptation of the word, for they are produced, not by orders verbally expressed, but by expressive movements. If the hands are opened and drawn close to the mouth, as when a kiss is wafted, the mouth smiles. If the arms are extended and half bent at the elbows, the countenance assumes an expression of astonishment. The slightest variation of movement is reflected in the emotions. If the fists are closed, the brow contracts and the face expresses anger. If a lively or sad tune is played, if amusing or depressing pictures are shown, the subject, like a faithful mirror, at once reflects these impressions. If a smile is produced it can be seen to diminish and disappear at the same time as the hand is moved away, and again to reappear and increase when it is once more brought near. Better still, a double expression can be imparted to the physiognomy, by approaching the left hand to the left side of the mouth, the left side of the physiognomy will smile, while at the same time, by closing the right hand, the right eyebrow will frown. The subject can be made to send kisses, or to turn his hands round each other indefinitely. If the hand is brought near the nose it will blow; if the arms are stretched out they will remain extended, while the head will be bowed with a marked expression of pain."

Heidenhain was able to take possession of the subject's gaze and control him by sight, through producing mimicry. He looks fixedly at the patient till the patient is unable to take his eyes away. Then the patient will copy every movement he makes. If he rises and goes backward the patient will follow, and with his right hand he will imitate the movements of the operator's left, as if he were a mirror. The attitudes of prayer, melancholy, pain, disdain, anger or fear, may be produced in this manner.

The experiments of Donato, a stage hypnotizer, are thus described: "After throwing the subjects into catalepsy he causes soft music to be played, which produces a rapturous expression. If the sound is heightened or increased, the subjects seem to receive a shock and a feeling of disappointment. The artistic sense developed by hypnotism is disturbed; the faces express astonishment, stupefaction and pain. If the same soft melody be again resumed, the same expression of rapturous bliss reappears in the countenance. The faces become seraphic and celestial when the subjects are by nature handsome, and when the subjects are ordinary looking, even ugly, they are idealized as by a special kind of beauty."

The strange part of all this is, that on awaking, the patient has no recollection of what has taken place, and careful tests have shown that what appear to be violent emotions, such as in an ordinary state would produce a quickened pulse and heavy breathing, create no disturbance whatever in the cataleptic subject; only the outer mask is in motion.

"Sometimes the subjects lean backward with all the grace of a perfect equilibrist, freeing themselves from the ordinary mechanical laws. The curvature will, indeed, at times be so complete that the head will touch the floor and the body describe a regular arc.

"When a female subject assumes an attitude of devotion, clasps her hands, turns her eyes upward and lisps out a prayer, she presents an admirably artistic picture, and her features and expression seem worthy of being reproduced on canvas."

We thus see what a perfect automaton the human body may become. There appears, however, to be a sort of unconscious memory, for a familiar object will seem to suggest spontaneously its ordinary use. Thus, if a piece of soap is put into a cataleptic patient's hands; he will move it around as though he thought he were washing them, and if there is any water near he will actually wash them. The sight of an umbrella makes him shiver as if he were in a storm. Handing such a person a pen will not make him write, but if a letter is dictated to him out loud he will write in an irregular hand. The subject may also be made to sing, scream or speak different languages with which he is entirely unfamiliar. This is, however, a verging toward the somnambulistic stage, for in deep catalepsy the patient does not speak or hear. The state is produced by placing the hands on the head, the forehead, or nape of the neck.

THE SOMNAMBULISTIC STAGE.

This is the stage or phase of hypnotism nearest the waking, and is the only one that can be produced in some subjects. Patients in the cataleptic state can be brought into the somnambulistic by rubbing the top of the head. To all appearances, the patient is fully awake, his eyes are open, and he answers when spoken to, but his voice does not have the same sound as when awake. Yet, in this state the patient is susceptible of all the hallucinations of insanity which may be induced at the verbal command of the operator.

One of the most curious features of this stage of hypnotism is the effect on the memory. Says Monsieur Richet: "I send V------ to sleep. I recite some verses to her, and then I awake her. She remembers nothing. I again send her to sleep, and she remembers perfectly the verses I recited. I awake her, and she has again forgotten everything."

It appears, however, that if commanded to remember on awaking, a patient may remember.

The active sense, and the memory as well, appears to be in an exalted state of activity during this phase of hypnotism. Says M. Richet: "M---- -, who will sing the air of the second act of the Africaine in her sleep, is incapable of remembering a single note of it when awake." Another patient, while under this hypnotic influence, could remember all he had eaten for several days past, but when awake could remember very little. Binet and Fere caused one of their subjects to remember the whole of his repasts for eight days past, though when awake he could remember nothing beyond two or three days. A patient of Dr. Charcot, who when she was two years old had seen Dr. Parrot in the children's hospital, but had not seen him since, and when awake could not remember him, named him at once when he entered during her hypnotic sleep. M. Delboeuf tells of an experiment he tried, in which the patient did remember what had taken place during the hypnotic condition, when he suddenly awakened her in the midst of the hallucination; as, for instance, he told her the ashes from the cigar he was smoking had fallen on her handkerchief and had set it on fire, whereupon she at once rose and threw the handkerchief into the water. Then, suddenly awakened, she remembered the whole performance.

In the somnambulistic stage the patient is no longer an automaton merely, but a real personality, "an individual with his own character, his likes and dislikes." The tone of the voice of the operator seems to have quite as much effect as his words. If he speaks in a grave and solemn tone, for instance, even if what he utters is nonsense, the effect is that of a deeply tragic story.

The will of another is not so easily implanted as has been claimed. While a patient will follow almost any suggestion that may be offered, he readily obeys only commands which are in keeping with his character. If he is commanded to do something he dislikes or which in the waking state would be very repugnant to him, he hesitates, does it very reluctantly, and in extreme cases refuses altogether, often going into hysterics. It was found at the Charity hospital that one patient absolutely refused to accept a cassock and become a priest. One of Monsieur Richet's patients screamed with pain the moment an amputation was suggested, but almost immediately recognized that it was only a suggestion, and laughed in the midst of her tears. Probably, however, this patient was not completely hypnotized.

Dr. Dumontpallier was able to produce a very curious phenomenon. He suggested to a female patient that with the right eye she could see a picture on a blank card. On awakening she could, indeed, see the picture with the right eye, but the left eye told her the card was blank. While she was in the somnambulistic state he told her in her right ear that the weather was very fine, and at the same time another person whispered in her left ear that it was raining. On the right side of her face she had a smile, while the left angle of her lip dropped as if she were depressed by the thought of the rain. Again, he describes a dance and gay party in one ear, and another person mimics the barking of a dog in the other. One side of her face in that case wears an amused expression, while the other shows signs of alarm.

Dr. Charcot thus describes a curious experiment: "A portrait is suggested to a subject as existing on a blank card, which is then mixed with a dozen others; to all appearance they are similar cards. The subject, being awakened, is requested to look over the packet, and does so without knowing the reason of the request, but when he perceives the card on which the portrait was suggested, he at once recognizes the imaginary portrait. It is probable that some insignificant mark has, owing to his visual hyperacuity, fixed the image in the subject's brain."

FASCINATION.

Says a recent French writer: "Dr. Bremand, a naval doctor, has obtained in men supposed to be perfectly healthy a new condition, which he calls fascination. The inventor considers that this is hypnotism in its mildest form, which, after repeated experiments, might become catalepsy. The subject fascinated by Dr. Bremaud--fascination being induced by the contemplation of a bright spot--falls into a state of stupor. He follows the operator and servilely imitates his movements, gestures and words; he obeys suggestions, and a stimulation of the nerves induces contraction, but the cataleptic pliability does not exist."

A noted public hypnotizer in Paris some years ago produced fascination in the following manner: He would cause the subject to lean on his hands, thus fatiguing the muscles. The excitement produced by the concentrated gaze of a large audience also assisted in weakening the nervous resistance. At last the operator would suddenly call out: "Look at me!" The subject would look up and gaze steadily into the operator's eyes, who would stare steadily back with round, glaring eyes, and in most cases subdue his victim.

CHAPTER IV.

How the Subject Feels Under Hypnotization.--Dr. Cooper's Experience.--Effect of Music.--Dr. Alfred Marthieu's Experiments.

The sensations produced during a state of hypnosis are very interesting. As may be supposed, they differ greatly in different persons. One of the most interesting accounts ever given is that of Dr. James R. Cocke, a hypnotist himself, who submitted to being operated upon by a professional magnetizer. He was at that time a firm believer in the theory of personal magnetism (a delusion from which he afterward escaped).

On the occasion which he describes, the operator commanded him to close his eyes and told him he could not open them, but he did open them at once. Again he told him to close the eyes, and at the same time he gently stroked his head and face and eyelids with his hand. Dr. Cocke fancied he felt a tingling sensation in his forehead and eyes, which he supposed came from the hand of the operator. (Afterward he came to believe that this sensation was purely imaginary on his part.)

Then he says: "A sensation akin to fear came over me. The operator said: 'You are going to sleep, you are getting sleepy. You cannot open your eyes.' I was conscious that my heart was beating rapidly, and I felt a sensation of terror. He continued to tell me I was going to sleep, and could not open my eyes. He then made passes over my head, down over my hands and body, but did not touch me. He then said to me, 'You cannot open your eyes.' The motor apparatus of my lids would not seemingly respond to my will, yet I was conscious that while one part of my mind wanted to open my eyes, another part did not want to, so I was in a paradoxical state. I believed that I could open my eyes, and yet could not. The feeling of not wishing to open my eyes was not based upon any desire to please the operator. I had no personal interest in him in any way, but, be it understood, I firmly believed in his power to control me. He continued to suggest to me that I was going to sleep, and the suggestion of terror previously mentioned continued to increase."

The next step was to put the doctor's hand over his head, and tell him he could not put it down. Then he stroked the arm and said it was growing numb. He said: "You have no feeling in it, have you?" Dr. Cocke goes on: "I said 'No,' and I knew that I said 'No,' yet I knew that I had a feeling in it." The operator went on, pricking the arm with a pin, and though Dr. Cocke felt the pain he said he did not feel it, and at the same time the sensation of terror increased. "I was not conscious of my body at all," he says further on, "but I was painfully conscious of the two contradictory elements within me. I knew that my body existed, but could not prove it to myself. I knew that the statements made by the operator were in a measure untrue. I obeyed them voluntarily and involuntarily. This is the last remembrance that I have of that hypnotic experience."

After this, however, the operator caused the doctor to do a number of things which he learned of from his friends after the performance was over. "It seemed to me that the hypnotist commanded me to awake as soon as I dropped my arm," and yet ten minutes of unconsciousness had passed.

On a subsequent occasion Dr. Cocke, who was blind, was put into a deep hypnotic sleep by fixing his mind on the number 26 and holding up his hand. This time he experienced a still greater degree of terror, and incidentally learned that he could hypnotize himself. The matter of self-hypnotism we shall consider in another chapter.

In this connection we find great interest in an article in the Medical News, July 28, 1894, by Dr. Alfred Warthin, of Ann Arbor, Mich., in which he describes the effects of music upon hypnotic subjects. While in Vienna he took occasion to observe closely the enthusiastic musical devotees as they sat in the audience at the performance of one of Wagner's operas. He believed they were in a condition of self-induced hypnotism, in which their subjective faculties were so exalted as to supersede their objective perceptions. Music was no longer to them a succession of pleasing sounds, but the embodiment of a drama in which they became so wrapped up that they forgot all about the mechanical and external features of the music and lived completely in a fairy world of dream.

This observation suggested to him an interesting series of experiments. His first subject was easily hypnotized, and of an emotional nature. Wagner's "Ride of Walkure" was played from the piano score. The pulse of the subject became more rapid and at first of higher tension, increasing from a normal rate of 60 beats a minute to 120. Then, as the music progressed, the tension diminished. The respiration increased from 18 to 30 per minute. Great excitement in the subject was evident. His whole body was thrown into motion, his legs were drawn up, his arms tossed into the air, and a profuse sweat appeared. When the subject had been awakened, he said that he did not remember the music as music, but had an impression of intense, excitement, brought on by "riding furiously through the air." The state of mind brought up before him in the most realistic and vivid manner possible the picture of the ride of Tam O'Shanter, which he had seen years before. The picture soon became real to him, and he found himself taking part in a wild chase, not as witch, devil, or Tam even; but in some way his consciousness was spread through every part of the scene, being of it, and yet playing the part of spectator, as is often the case in dreams.

Dr. Warthin tried the same experiment again, this time on a young man who was not so emotional, and was hypnotized with much more difficulty. This subject did not pass into such a deep state of hypnotism, but the result was practically the same. The pulse rate rose from 70 to 120. The sensation remembered was that of riding furiously through the air.

The experiment was repeated on other subjects, in all cases with the same result. Only one knew that the music was the "Ride of Walkure." "To him it always expressed the pictured wild ride of the daughters of Wotan, the subject taking part in the ride." It was noticeable in each case that the same music played to them in the waking state produced no special impression. Here is incontestable evidence that in the hypnotic state the perception of the special senses is enormously heightened.

A slow movement was tried (the Valhalla motif). At first it seemed to produce the opposite effect, for the pulse was lowered. Later it rose to a rate double the normal, and the tension was diminished. The impression described by the subject afterward was a feeling of "lofty grandeur and calmness." A mountain climbing experience of years before was recalled, and the subject seemed to contemplate a landscape of "lofty grandeur." A different sort of music was played (the intense and ghastly scene in which Brunhilde appears to summon Sigmund to Valhalla). Immediately a marked change took place in the pulse. It became slow and irregular, and very small. The respiration decreased almost to gasping, the face grew pale, and a cold perspiration broke out.

Readers who are especially interested in this subject will find descriptions of many other interesting experiments in the same article.

Dr. Cocke describes a peculiar trick he played upon the sight of a subject. Says he: "I once hypnotized a man and made him read all of his a's as w's, his u's as v's, and his b's as x's. I added suggestion after suggestion so rapidly that it would have been impossible for him to have remembered simply what I said and call the letters as I directed. Stimulation was, in this case impossible, as I made him read fifteen or twenty pages, he calling the letters as suggested each time they occurred."

The extraordinary heightening of the sense perceptions has an important bearing on the question of spiritualism and clairvoyance. If the powers of the mind are so enormously increased, all that is required of a very sensitive and easily hypnotized person is to hypnotize him or herself, when he will be able to read thoughts and remember or perceive facts hidden to the ordinary perception. In this connection the reader is referred to the confession of Mrs. Piper, the famous medium of the American branch of the Psychical Research Society. The confession will be found printed in full at the close of this book.

CHAPTER V.

Self-Hypnotization.--How It may Be Done.--An Experience.--Accountable for Children's Crusade.--Oriental Prophets Self-Hypnotized.

If self-hypnotism is possible (and it is true that a person can deliberately hypnotize himself when he wishes to till he has become accustomed to it and is expert in it, so to speak), it does away at a stroke with the claims of all professional hypnotists and magnetic healers that they have any peculiar power in themselves which they exert over their fellows. One of these professionals gives an account in his book of what he calls "The Wonderful Lock Method." He says that though he is locked up in a separate room he can make the psychic power work through the walls. All that he does is to put his subjects in the way of hypnotizing themselves. He shows his inconsistency when he states that under certain circumstances the hypnotizer is in danger of becoming hypnotized himself. In this he makes no claim that the subject is using any psychic power; but, of course, if the hypnotizer looks steadily into the eyes of his subject, and the subject looks into his eyes, the steady gaze on a bright object will produce hypnotism in one quite as readily as in the other.

Hypnotism is an established scientific fact; but the claim that the hypnotizer has any mysterious psychic power is the invariable mark of the charlatan. Probably no scientific phenomenon was ever so grossly prostituted to base ends as that of hypnotism. Later we shall see some of the outrageous forms this charlatanism assumes, and how it extends to the professional subjects as well as to the professional operators, till those subjects even impose upon scientific men who ought to be proof against such deception. Moreover, the possibility of self-hypnotization, carefully concealed and called by another name, opens another great field of humbug and charlatanism, of which the advertising columns of the newspapers are constantly filled--namely, that of the clairvoyant and medium. We may conceive how such a profession might become perfectly legitimate and highly useful; but at present it seems as if any person who went into it, however honest he might be at the start, soon began to deceive himself as well as others, until he lost his power entirely to distinguish between fact and imagination.

Before discussing the matter further, let us quote Dr. Cocke's experiment in hypnotizing himself. It will be remembered that a professional hypnotizer or magnetizer had hypnotized him by telling him to fix his mind on the number twenty-six and holding up his hand. Says the doctor:

"In my room that evening it occurred to me to try the same experiment. I did so. I kept the number twenty-six in my mind. In a few minutes I felt the sensation of terror, but in a different way. I was intensely cold. My heart seemed to stand still. I had ringing in my ears. My hair seemed to rise upon my scalp. I persisted in the effort, and the previously mentioned noise in my ears grew louder and louder. The roar became deafening. It crackled like a mighty fire. I was fearfully conscious of myself. Having read vivid accounts of dreams, visions, etc.

, it occurred to me that I would experience them. I felt in a vague way that there were beings all about me but could not hear their voices. I felt as though every muscle in my body was fixed and rigid. The roar in my ears grew louder still, and I heard, above the roar, reports which sounded like artillery and musketry. Then above the din of the noise a musical chord. I seemed to be absorbed in this chord. I knew nothing else. The world existed for me only in the tones of the mighty chord. Then I had a sensation as though I were expanding. The sound in my ears died away, and yet I was not conscious of silence. Then all consciousness was lost. The next thing I experienced was a sensation of intense cold, and of someone roughly shaking me. Then I heard the voice of my jolly landlord calling me by name."

The landlord had found the doctor "as white as a ghost and as limp as a rag," and thought he was dead. He says it took him ten minutes to arouse the sleeper. During the time a physician had been summoned.

As to the causes of this condition as produced Dr. Cocke says: "I firmly believed that something would happen when the attempt was made to hypnotize me. Secondly, I wished to be hypnotized. These, together with a vivid imagination and strained attention, brought on the states which occurred."

It is interesting to compare the effects of hypnotization with those of opium or other narcotic. Dr. Cocke asserts that there is a difference. His descriptions of dreams bear a wonderful likeness to De Quincey's dreams, such as those described in "The English Mail-Coach," "De Profundis," and "The Confessions of an English Opium Eater," all of which were presumably due to opium.

The causes which Dr. Cocke thinks produced the hypnotic condition in his case, namely, belief, desire to be hypnotized, and strained attention, united with a vivid imagination, are causes which are often found in conjunction and produce effects which we may reasonably explain on the theory of self-hypnotization.

For instance, the effects of an exciting religious revival are very like those produced by Mesmer's operations in Paris. The subjects become hysterical, and are ready to believe anything or do anything. By prolonging the operation, a whole community becomes more or less hypnotized. In all such cases, however, unusual excitement is commonly followed by unusual lethargy. It is much like a wild spree of intoxication--in fact, it is a sort of intoxication.

The same phenomena are probably accountable for many of the strange records of history. The wonderful cures at Lourdes (of which we have read in Zola's novel of that name) are no doubt the effect of hypnotization by the priests. Some of the strange movements of whole communities during the Crusades are to be explained either on the theory of hypnotization or of contagion, and possibly these two things will turn out to be much the same in fact. On no other ground can we explain the so-called "Children's Crusade," in which over thirty thousand children from Germany, from all classes of the community, tried to cross the Alps in winter, and in their struggles were all lost or sold into slavery without even reaching the Holy Land.

Again, hypnotism is accountable for many of the poet's dreams. Gazing steadily at a bed of bright coals or a stream of running water will invariably throw a sensitive subject into a hypnotic sleep that will last sometimes for several hours. Dr. Cocke says that he has experimented in this direction with patients of his. Says he: "They have the ability to resist the state or to bring it at will. Many of them describe beautiful scenes from nature, or some mighty cathedral with its lofty dome, or the faces of imaginary beings, beautiful or demoniacal, according to the will and temper of the subject."

Perhaps the most wonderful example of self-hypnotism which we have in history is that of the mystic Swedenborg, who saw, such strange things in his visions, and at last came to believe in them as real.

The same explanation may be given of the manifestations of Oriental prophets--for in the Orient hypnotism is much easier and more systematically developed than with us of the West. The performances of the dervishes, and also of the fakirs, who wound themselves and perform many wonderful feats which would be difficult for an ordinary person, are no doubt in part feats of hypnotism.

While in a condition of auto-hypnotization a person may imagine that he is some other personality. Says Dr. Cocke: "A curious thing about those self-hypnotized subjects is that they carry out perfectly their own ideals of the personality with whom they believe themselves to be possessed. If their own ideals of the part they are playing are imperfect, their impersonations are ridiculous in the extreme. One man I remember believed himself to be controlled by the spirit of Charles Sumner. Being uneducated, he used the most wretched English, and his language was utterly devoid of sense. While, on the other hand, a very intelligent lady who believed herself to be controlled by the spirit of Charlotte Cushman personated the part very well."

Dr. Cooke says of himself: "I can hypnotize myself to such an extent that I will become wholly unconscious of events taking place around me, and a long interval of time, say from one-half to two hours, will be a complete blank. During this condition of auto-hypnotization I will obey suggestions made to me by another, talking rationally, and not knowing any event that has occurred after the condition has passed off."

CHAPTER VI.

Simulation.--Deception in Hypnotism Very Common.--Examples of Neuropathic Deceit.--Detecting Simulation. --Professional Subjects.--How Dr. Luys of the Charity Hospital at Paris Was Deceived.--Impossibility of Detecting Deception in All Cases.--Confessions of a Professional Hypnotic Subject.

It has already been remarked that hypnotism and hysteria are conditions very nearly allied, and that hysterical neuropathic individuals make the best hypnotic subjects. Now persons of this character are in most cases morally as well as physically degenerate, and it is a curious fact that deception seems to be an inherent element in nearly all such characters. Expert doctors have been thoroughly deceived. And again, persons who have been trying to expose frauds have also been deceived by the positive statements of such persons that they were deceiving the doctors when they were not. A diseased vanity seems to operate in such cases and the subjects take any method which promises for the time being to bring them into prominence. Merely to attract attention is a mania with some people.

There is also something about the study of hypnotism, and similar subjects in which delusions constitute half the existence, that seems to destroy the faculty for distinguishing between truth and delusion. Undoubtedly we must look on such manifestations as a species of insanity.

There is also a point at which the unconscious deceiver, for the sake of gain, passes into the conscious deceiver. At the close of this chapter we will give some cases illustrating the fact that persons may learn by practice to do seemingly impossible things, such as holding themselves perfectly rigid (as in the cataleptic state) while their head rests on one chair and their heels on another, and a heavy person sits upon them.

First, let us cite a few cases of what may be called neuropathic deceit--a kind of insanity which shows itself in deceiving. The newspapers record similar cases from time to time. The first two of the following are quoted by Dr. Courmelles from the French courts, etc.

1. The Comtesse de W-- accused her maid of having attempted to poison her. The case was a celebrated one, and the court-room was thronged with women who sympathized with the supposed victim. The maid was condemned to death; but a second trial was granted, at which it was conclusively proved that the Comtesse had herself bound herself on her bed, and had herself poured out the poison which was found still blackening her breast and lips.

2. In 1886 a man called Ulysse broke into the shop of a second-hand dealer, facing his own house in Paris, and there began deliberately to take away the goods, just as if he were removing his own furniture. This he did without hurrying himself in any way, and transported the property to his own premises. Being caught in the very act of the theft, he seemed at first to be flurried and bewildered. When arrested and taken to the lock-up, he seemed to be in a state of abstraction; when spoken to he made no reply, seemed ready to fall asleep, and when brought before the examining magistrate actually fell asleep. Dr. Garnier, the medical man attached to the infirmary of the police establishment, had no doubt of his irresponsibility and he was released from custody.

3. While engaged as police-court reporter for a Boston newspaper, the present writer saw a number of strange cases of the same kind. One was that of a quiet, refined, well educated lady, who was brought in for shop-lifting. Though her husband was well to do, and she did not sell or even use the things she took, she had made a regular business of stealing whenever she could. She had begun it about seven months before by taking a lace handkerchief, which she slipped under her shawl: Soon after she accomplished another theft. "I felt so encouraged," she said, "that I got a large bag, which I fastened under my dress, and into this I slipped whatever I could take when the clerks were not looking. I do not know what made me do it. My success seemed to lead me on."

Other cases of kleptomania could easily be cited.

"Simulation," say Messieurs Binet and Fere, "which is already a stumbling block in the study of hysterical cases, becomes far more formidable in such studies as we are now occupied with. It is only when he has to deal with physical phenomena that the operator feels himself on firm ground."

Yet even here we can by no means feel certain. Physicians have invented various ingenious pieces of apparatus for testing the circulation and other physiological conditions; but even these things are not sure tests. The writer knows of the case of a man who has such control over his heart and lungs that he can actually throw himself into a profound sleep in which the breathing is so absolutely stopped for an hour that a mirror is not moistened in the least by the breath, nor can the pulses be felt. To all intents and purposes the man appears to be dead; but in due time he comes to life again, apparently no whit the worse for his experiment.

If an ordinary person were asked to hold out his arms at full length for five minutes he would soon become exhausted, his breathing would quicken, his pulse-rate increase. It might be supposed that if these conditions did not follow the subject was in a hypnotic trance; but it is well known that persons may easily train themselves to hold out the arms for any length of time without increasing the respiration by one breath or raising the pulse rate at all. We all remember Montaigne's famous illustration in which he said that if a woman began by carrying a calf about every day she would still be able to carry it when it became an ox.

In the Paris hospitals, where the greater number of regular scientific experiments have been conducted, it is found that "trained subjects" are required for all of the more difficult demonstrations. That some of these famous scientists have been deceived, there is no doubt. They know it themselves. A case which will serve as an illustration is that of Dr. Luys, some of whose operations were "exposed" by Dr. Ernest Hart, an English student of hypnotism of a skeptical turn of mind. One of Dr. Luys's pupils in a book he has published makes the following statement, which helps to explain the circumstances which we will give a little later. Says he:

"We know that many hospital patients who are subjected to the higher or greater treatment of hypnotism are of very doubtful reputations; we know also the effects of a temperament which in them is peculiarly addicted to simulation, and which is exaggerated by the vicinity of maladies similar to their own. To judge of this, it is necessary to have seen them encourage each other in simulation, rehearsing among themselves, or even before the medical students of the establishment, the experiments to which they have been subjected; and going through their different contortions and attitudes to exercise themselves in them. And then, again, in the present day, has not the designation of an 'hypnotical subject' become almost a social position? To be fed, to be paid, admired, exhibited in public, run after, and all the rest of it--all this is enough to make the most impartial looker-on skeptical. But is it enough to enable us to produce an a priori negation? Certainly not; but it is sufficient to justify legitimate doubt. And when we come to moral phenomena, where we have to put faith in the subject, the difficulty becomes still greater. Supposing suggestion and hallucination to be granted, can they be demonstrated? Can we by plunging the subject in hypnotical sleep, feel sure of what he may affirm? That is impossible, for simulation and somnambulism are not reciprocally exclusive terms, and Monsieur Pitres has established the fact that a subject who sleeps may still simulate." Messieurs Binet and Fere in their book speak of "the honest Hublier, whom his somnambulist Emelie cheated for four years consecutively."

Let us now quote Mr. Hart's investigations.

Dr. Luys is an often quoted authority on hypnotism in Paris, and is at the head of what is called the Charity Hospital school of hypnotical experiments. In 1892 he announced some startling results, in which some people still have faith (more or less). What he was supposed to accomplish was stated thus in the London Pall Mall Gazette, issue of December 2: "Dr. Luys then showed us how a similar artificial state of suffering could be created without suggestion--in fact, by the mere proximity of certain substances. A pinch of coal dust, for example, corked and sealed in a small phial and placed by the side of the neck of a hypnotized person, produces symptoms of suffocation by smoke; a tube of distilled water, similarly placed, provokes signs of incipient hydrophobia; while another very simple concoction put in contact with the flesh brings on symptoms of suffocation by drowning."

Signs of drunkenness were said to be caused by a small corked bottle of brandy, and the nature of a cat by a corked bottle of valerian. Patients also saw beautiful blue flames about the north pole of a magnet and distasteful red flames about the south pole; while by means of a magnet it was said that the symptoms of illness of a sick patient might be transferred to a well person also in the hypnotic state, but of course on awaking the well person at once threw off sickness that had been transferred, but the sick person was permanently relieved. These experiments are cited in some recent books on hypnotism, apparently with faith. The following counter experiments will therefore be read with interest.

Dr. Hart gives a full account of his investigations in the Nineteenth Century. Dr. Luys gave Dr. Hart some demonstrations, which the latter describes as follows: "A tube containing ten drachms of cognac were placed at a certain point on the subject's neck, which Dr. Luys said was the seat of the great nerve plexuses. The effect on Marguerite was very rapid and marked; she began to move her lips and to swallow; the expression of her face changed, and she asked, 'What have you been giving me to drink? I am quite giddy.' At first she had a stupid and troubled look; then she began to get gay. 'I am ashamed of myself,' she said; 'I feel quite tipsy,' and after passing through some of the phases of lively inebriety she began to fall from the chair, and was with difficulty prevented from sprawling on the floor. She was uncomfortable, and seemed on the point of vomiting, but this was stopped, and she was calmed."

Another patient gave all the signs of imagining himself transformed into a cat when a small corked bottle of valerian was placed on his neck.

In the presence of a number of distinguished doctors in Paris, Dr. Hart tried a series of experiments in which by his conversation he gave the patient no clue to exactly what drug he was using, in order that if the patient was simulating he would not know what to simulate. Marguerite was the subject of several of these experiments, one of which is described as follows:

"I took a tube which was supposed to contain alcohol, but which did contain cherry laurel water. Marguerite immediately began, to use the words of M. Sajous's note, to smile agreeably and then to laugh; she became gay. 'It makes me laugh,' she said, and then, 'I'm not tipsy, I want to sing,' and so on through the whole performance of a not ungraceful giserie, which we stopped at that stage, for I was loth to have the degrading performance of drunkenness carried to the extreme I had seen her go through at the Charite. I now applied a tube of alcohol, asking the assistant, however, to give me valerian, which no doubt this profoundly hypnotized subject perfectly well heard, for she immediately went through the whole cat performance. She spat, she scratched, she mewed, she leapt about on all fours, and she was as thoroughly cat-like as had been Dr. Luys's subjects."

Similar experiments as to the effect of magnets and electric currents were tried. A note taken by Dr. Sajous runs thus: "She found the north pole, notwithstanding there was no current, very pretty; she was as if she were fascinated by it; she caressed the blue flames, and showed every sign of delight. Then came the phenomena of attraction. She followed the magnet with delight across the room, as though fascinated by it; the bar was turned so as to present the other end or what would be called, in the language of La Charite, the south pole. Then she fell into an attitude, of repulsion and horror, with clenched fists, and as it approached her she fell backward into the arms of M. Cremiere, and was carried, still showing all the signs of terror and repulsion, back to her chair. The bar was again turned until what should have been the north pole was presented to her. She again resumed the same attitudes of attraction, and tears bedewed her cheeks. 'Ah,' she said, 'it is blue, the flame mounts,' and she rose from her seat, following the magnet around the room. Similar but false phenomena were obtained in succession with all the different forms of magnet and non-magnet; Marguerite was never once right, but throughout her acting was perfect; she was utterly unable at any time really to distinguish between a plain bar of iron, demagnetized magnet or a horseshoe magnet carrying a full current and one from which the current was wholly cut off."

Five different patients were tested in the same way, through a long series of experiments, with the same results, a practical proof that Dr. Luys had been totally deceived and his new and wonderful discoveries amounted to nothing.

There is, however, another possible explanation, namely, telepathy, in a real hypnotic condition. Even if Dr. Luys's experiments were genuine this would be the rational explanation. They were a case of suggestion of some sort, without doubt.

Nearly every book on hypnotism gives various rules for detecting simulation of the hypnotic state. One of the commonest tests is that of anaesthesia. A pin or pen-knife is stuck into a subject to see if he is insensible to pain; but as we shall see in a latter chapter, this insensibility also may be simulated, for by long training some persons learn to control their facial expressions perfectly. We have already seen that the pulse and respiration tests are not sufficient. Hypnotic persons often flush slightly in the face; but it is true that there are persons who can flush on any part of the body at will.

Mr. Ernest Hart had an article in the Century Magazine on "The Eternal Gullible," in which he gives the confessions of a professional hypnotic subject. This person, whom he calls L., he brought to his house, where some experiments were tried in the presence of a number of doctors, whose names are quoted. The quotation of a paragraph or two from Mr. Hart's article will be of interest. Says he:

"The 'catalepsy business' had more artistic merit. So rigid did L. make his muscles that he could be lifted in one piece like an Egyptian mummy. He lay with his head on the back of one chair, and his heels on another, and allowed a fairly heavy man to sit on his stomach; it seemed to me, however, that he was here within a 'straw' or two of the limit of his endurance. The 'blister trick,' spoken of by Truth as having deceived some medical men, was done by rapidly biting and sucking the skin of the wrist. L. did manage with some difficulty to raise a slight swelling, but the marks of the teeth were plainly visible." (Possibly L. had made his skin so tough by repeated biting that he could no longer raise the blister!)

"One point in L.'s exhibition which was undoubtedly genuine was his remarkable and stoical endurance of pain. He stood before us smiling and open-eyed while he ran long needles into the fleshy part of his arms and legs without flinching, and he allowed one of the gentlemen present to pinch his skin in different parts with strong crenated pincers in a manner which bruised it, and which to most people would have caused intense pain. L. allowed no sign of suffering or discomfort to appear; he did not set his teeth or wince; his pulse was not quickened, and the pupil of his eye did not dilate as physiologists tell us it does when pain passes a certain limit. It may be said that this merely shows that in L. the limit of endurance was beyond the normal standard; or, in other words, that his sensitiveness was less than that of the average man. At any rate his performance in this respect was so remarkable that some of the gentlemen present were fain to explain it by supposed 'post- hypnotic suggestion,' the theory apparently being that L. and his comrades hypnotized one another, and thus made themselves insensible to pain.

"As surgeons have reason to know, persons vary widely in their sensitiveness to pain. I have seen a man chat quietly with bystanders while his carotid artery was being tied without the use of chloroform. During the Russo-Turkish war wounded Turks often astonished English doctors by undergoing the most formidable amputations with no other anaesthetic than a cigarette. Hysterical women will inflict very severe pain on themselves--merely for wantonness or in order to excite sympathy. The fakirs who allow themselves to be hung up by hooks beneath their shoulder-blades seem to think little of it and, as a matter of fact, I believe are not much inconvenienced by the process."

The fact is, the amateur can always be deceived, and there are no special tests that can be relied on. If a person is well accustomed to hypnotic manifestations, and also a good judge of human nature, and will keep constantly on guard, using every precaution to avoid deception, it is altogether likely that it can be entirely obviated. But one must use his good judgment in every possible way. In the case of fresh subjects, or persons well known, of course there is little possibility of deception. And the fact that deception exists does not in any way invalidate the truth of hypnotism as a scientific phenomenon. We cite it merely as one of the physiological peculiarities connected with the mental condition of which it is a manifestation. The fact that a tendency to deception exists is interesting in itself, and may have an influence upon our judgment of our fellow beings. There is, to be sure, a tendency on the part of scientific writers to find lunatics instead of criminals; but knowledge of the well demonstrated fact that many criminals are insane helps to make us charitable.

CHAPTER VII.

Criminal Suggestion.--Laboratory Crimes.--Dr. Cocke's Experiments Showing Criminal Suggestion Is not Possible.--Dr. William James' Theory. --A Bad Man Cannot Be Made Good, Why Expect to Make a Good Man Bad?

One of the most interesting phases of hypnotism is that of post-hypnotic suggestion, to which reference has already been made. It is true that a suggestion made during the hypnotic condition as to what a person will do after coming out of the hypnotic sleep may be carried out. A certain professional hypnotizer claims that once he has hypnotized a person he can keep that person forever after under his influence by means of post-hypnotic suggestion. He says to him while in the hypnotic sleep: "Whenever I look at you, or point at you, you will fall asleep. No one can hypnotize you but me. Whenever I try to hypnotize you, you will fall asleep." He says further: "Suggest to a subject while he is sound asleep that in eight weeks he will mail you a letter with a blank piece of note paper inside, and during the intervening period you may yourself forget the occurrence, but in exactly eight weeks he will carry out the suggestion. Suggestions of this nature are always carried out, especially when the suggestion is to take effect on some certain day or date named. Suggest to a subject that in ninety days from a given date he will come to your house with his coat on inside out, and he will most certainly do so."

The same writer also definitely claims that he can hypnotize people against their wills. If this were true, what a terrible power would a shrewd, evil-minded criminal have to compel the execution of any of his plans! We hope to show that it is not true; but we must admit that many scientific men have tried experiments which they believe demonstrate beyond a doubt that criminal use can be and is made of hypnotic influence. If it were possible to make a person follow out any line of conduct while actually under hypnotic influence it would be bad enough; but the use of posthypnotic suggestion opens a yet more far-reaching and dangerous avenue.

Among the most definite claims of the evil deeds that may be compelled during hypnotic sleep is that of Dr. Luys, whom we have already seen as being himself deceived by professional hypnotic subjects. Says he: "You cannot only oblige this defenseless being, who is incapable of opposing the slightest resistance, to give from hand to hand anything you may choose, but you can also make him sign a promise, draw up a bill of exchange, or any other kind of agreement. You may make him write an holographic will (which according to French law would be valid), which he will hand over to you, and of which he will never know the existence. He is ready to fulfill the minutest legal formalities, and will do so with a calm, serene and natural manner calculated to deceive the most expert law officers. These somnambulists will not hesitate either, you may be sure, to make a denunciation, or to bear false witness; they are, I repeat, the passive instruments of your will. For instance, take E. She will at my bidding write out and sign a donation of forty pounds in my favor. In a criminal point of view the subject under certain suggestions will make false denunciations, accuse this or that person, and maintain with the greatest assurance that he has assisted at an imaginary crime. I will recall to your mind those scenes of fictitious assassination, which have exhibited before you. I was careful to place in the subject's hands a piece of paper instead of a dagger or a revolver; but it is evident, that if they had held veritable murderous instruments, the scene might have had a tragic ending."

Many experiments along this line have been tried, such as suggesting the theft of a watch or a spoon, which afterward was actually carried out.

It may be said at once that "these laboratory crimes" are in most cases successful: A person who has nothing will give away any amount if told to do so; but quite different is the case of a wealthy merchant who really has money to sign away.

Dr. Cocke describes one or two experiments of his own which have an important bearing on the question of criminal suggestion. Says he: "A girl who was hypnotized deeply was given a glass of water and was told that it was a lighted lamp. A broomstick was placed across the room and she was told that it was a man who intended to injure her. I suggested to her that she throw the glass of water (she supposing it was a lighted lamp) at the broomstick, her enemy, and she immediately threw it with much violence. Then a man was placed across the room, and she was given instead of a glass of water a lighted lamp. I told her that the lamp was a glass of water, and that the man across the room was her brother. It was suggested to her that his clothing was on fire and she was commanded to extinguish the fire by throwing the lighted lamp at the individual, she having been told, as was previously mentioned, that it was a glass of water. Without her knowledge a person was placed behind her for the purpose of quickly checking her movements, if desired. I then commanded her to throw the lamp at the man. She raised the lamp, hesitated, wavered, and then became very hysterical, laughing and crying alternately. This condition was so profound that she came very near dropping the lamp. Immediately after she was quieted I made a number of tests to prove that she was deeply hypnotized. Standing in front of her I gave her a piece of card-board, telling her that it was a dagger, and commanded her to stab me. She immediately struck at me with the piece of card-board. I then gave her an open pocketknife and commanded her to strike at me with it. Again she raised it to execute my command, again hesitated, and had another hysterical attack. I have tried similar experiments with thirty or forty people with similar results. Some of them would have injured themselves severely, I am convinced, at command, but to what extent I of course cannot say. That they could have been induced to harm others, or to set fire to houses, etc., I do not believe. I say this after very careful reading and a large amount of experimentation."

Dr. Cocke also declares his belief that no person can be hypnotized against his will by a person who is repugnant to him.

The facts in the case are probably those that might be indicated by a common-sense consideration of the conditions. If a person is weak-minded and susceptible to temptation, to theft, for instance, no doubt a familiar acquaintance of a similar character might hypnotize that person and cause him to commit the crime to which his moral nature is by no means averse. If, on the other hand, the personality of the hypnotizer and the crime itself are repugnant to the hypnotic subject, he will absolutely refuse to do as he is bidden, even while in the deepest hypnotic sleep. On this point nearly all authorities agree.

Again, there is absolutely no well authenticated case of crime committed by a person under hypnotic influence. There have been several cases reported, and one woman in Paris who aided in a murder was released on her plea of irresponsibility because she had been hypnotized. In none of these cases, however, was there any really satisfactory evidence that hypnotism existed. In all the cases reported there seemed to be no doubt of the weak character and predisposition to crime. In another class of cases, namely those of criminal assault upon girls and women, the only evidence ever adduced that the injured person was hypnotized was the statement of that person, which cannot really be called evidence at all.

The fact is, a weak character can be tempted and brought under virtual control much more easily by ordinary means than by hypnotism. The man who "overpersuades" a business man to endorse a note uses no hypnotic influence. He is merely making a clever play upon the man's vanity, egotism, or good nature.

A profound study of the hypnotic state, such as has been made by Prof. William James, of Harvard College, the great authority on psychical phenomena and president of the Psychic Research Society, leads to the conviction that in the hypnotic sleep the will is only in abeyance, as it is in natural slumber or in sleepwalking, and any unusual or especially exciting occurrence, especially anything that runs against the grain of the nature, reawakens that will, and it soon becomes as active as ever. This is ten times more true in the matter of post- hypnotic suggestion, which is very much weaker than suggestion that takes effect during the actual hypnotic sleep. We shall see, furthermore, that while acting under a delusion at the suggestion of the operator, the patient is really conscious all the time of the real facts in the case--indeed, much more keenly so, oftentimes, than the operator himself. For instance, if a line is drawn on a sheet of paper and the subject is told there is no line, he will maintain there is no line; but he has to see it in order to ignore it. Moreover, persons trained to obey, instinctively do obey even in their waking state. It requires a special faculty to resist obedience, even during our ordinary waking condition. Says a recent writer: "It is certain that we are naturally inclined to obey, conflicts and resistance are the characteristics of some rare individuals; but between admitting this and saying that we are doomed to obey--even the least of us--lies a gulf." The same writer says further: "Hypnotic suggestion is an order given for a few seconds, at most a few minutes, to an individual in a state of induced sleep. The suggestion may be repeated; but it is absolutely powerless to transform a criminal into an honest man, or vice versa. " Here is an excellent argument. If it is possible to make criminals it should be quite as easy to make honest men. It is true that the weak are sometimes helped for good; but there is no case on record in which a person who really wished to be bad was ever made good; and the history of hypnotism is full of attempts in that direction. A good illustration is an experiment tried by Colonel de Rochas:

"An excellent subject * * * had been left alone for a few minutes in an apartment, and had stolen a valuable article. After he had left, the theft was discovered. A few days after it was suggested to the subject, while asleep, that he should restore the stolen object; the command was energetically and imperatively reiterated, but in vain. The theft had been committed by the subject, who had sold the article to an old curiosity dealer, as it was eventually found on information received from a third party. Yet this subject would execute all the imaginary crimes he was ordered."

As to the value of the so-called "laboratory crimes," the statement of Dr. Courmelles is of interest: "I have heard a subject say," he states, "'If I were ordered to throw myself out of the window I should do it, so certain am I either that there would be somebody under the window to catch me or that I should be stopped in time. The experimentalist's own interests and the consequences of such an act are a sure guarantee.'"

CHAPTER VIII.

Dangers in Being Hypnotized.--Condemnation of Public Performances.--A Common Sense View.--Evidence Furnished by Lafontaine.--By Dr. Courmelles.--By. Dr. Hart.--By Dr. Cocke.--No Danger in Hypnotism if Rightly Used by Physicians or Scientists.

Having considered the dangers to society through criminal hypnotic suggestion, let us now consider what dangers there may be to the individual who is hypnotized.

Before citing evidence, let us consider the subject from a rational point of view. Several things have already been established. We know that hypnotism is akin to hysteria and other forms of insanity--it is, in short, a kind of experimental insanity. Really good hypnotic subjects have not a perfect mental balance. We have also seen that repetition of the process increases the susceptibility, and in some cases persons frequently hypnotized are thrown into the hypnotic state by very slight physical agencies, such as looking at a bright doorknob. Furthermore, we know that the hypnotic patient is in a very sensitive condition, easily impressed. Moreover, it is well known that exertions required of hypnotic subjects are nervously very exhausting, so much so that headache frequently follows.

From these facts any reasonable person may make a few clear deductions. First, repeated strain of excitement in hypnotic seances will wear out the constitution just as certainly as repeated strain of excitement in social life, or the like, which, as we know, frequently produces nervous exhaustion. Second, it is always dangerous to submit oneself to the influence of an inferior or untrustworthy person. This is just as true in hypnotism as it is in the moral realm. Bad companions corrupt. And since the hypnotic subject is in a condition especially susceptible, a little association of this kind, a little submission to the inferior or immoral, will produce correspondingly more detrimental consequences. Third, since hypnotism is an abnormal condition, just as drunkenness is, one should not allow a public hypnotizer to experiment upon one and make one do ridiculous things merely for amusement, any more than one would allow a really insane person to be exhibited for money; or than one would allow himself to be made drunk, merely that by his absurd antics he might amuse somebody. It takes little reflection to convince any one that hypnotism for amusement, either on the public stage or in the home, is highly obnoxious, even if it is not highly dangerous. If the hypnotizer is an honest man, and a man of character, little injury may follow. But we can never know that, and the risk of getting into bad hands should prevent every one from submitting to influence at all. The fact is, however, that we should strongly doubt the good character of any one who hypnotizes for amusement, regarding him in the same light as we would one who intoxicated people on the stage for amusement, or gave them chloroform, or went about with a troup of insane people that he might exhibit their idiosyncrasies. Honest, right-minded people do not do those things.

At the same time, there is nothing wiser that a man can do than to submit himself fully to a stronger and wiser nature than his own. A physician in whom you have confidence may do a thousand times more for you by hypnotism than by the use of drugs. It is a safe rule to place hypnotism in exactly the same category as drugs. Rightly used, drugs are invaluable; wrongly used, they become the instruments of the murderer. At all times should they be used with great caution. The same is true of hypnotism.

Now let us cite some evidence. Lafontaine, a professional hypnotist, gives some interesting facts. He says that public hypnotic entertainments usually induce a great many of the audience to become amateur hypnotists, and these experiments may cause suffocation. Fear often results in congestion, or a rush of blood to the brain. "If the digestion is not completed, more especially if the repast has been more abundant than usual, congestion may be produced and death be instantaneous. The most violent convulsions may result from too complete magnetization of the brain. A convulsive movement may be so powerful that the body will suddenly describe a circle, the head touching the heels and seem to adhere to them. In this latter case there is torpor without sleep. Sometimes it has been impossible to awake the subject."

A waiter at Nantes, who was magnetized by a commercial traveler, remained for two days in a state of lethargy, and for three hours Dr. Foure and numerous spectators were able to verify that "the extremities were icy cold, the pulse no longer throbbed, the heart had no pulsations, respiration had ceased, and there was not sufficient breath to dim a glass held before the mouth. Moreover, the patient was stiff, his eyes were dull and glassy." Nevertheless, Lafontaine was able to recall this man to life.

Dr. Courmelles says: "Paralysis of one or more members, or of the tongue, may follow the awakening. These are the effects of the contractions of the internal muscles, due often to almost imperceptible touches. The diaphragm--and therefore the respiration--may be stopped in the same manner. Catalepsy and more especially lethargy, produce these phenomena."

There are on record a number of cases of idiocy, madness, and epilepsy caused by the unskillful provoking of hypnotic sleep. One case is sufficiently interesting, for it is almost exactly similar to a case that occurred at one of the American colleges. The subject was a young professor at a boys' school. "One evening he was present at some public experiments that were being performed in a tavern; he was in no way upset at the sight, but the next day one of his pupils, looking at him fixedly, sent him to sleep. The boys soon got into the habit of amusing themselves by sending him to sleep, and the unhappy professor had to leave the school, and place himself under the care of a doctor."

Dr. Ernest Hart gives an experience of his own which carries with it its own warning. Says he:

"Staying at the well known country house in Kent of a distinguished London banker, formerly member of Parliament for Greenwich, I had been called upon to set to sleep, and to arrest a continuous barking cough from which a young lady who was staying in the house was suffering, and who, consequently, was a torment to herself and her friends. I thought this a good opportunity for a control experiment, and I sat her down in front of a lighted candle which I assured her that I had previously mesmerized. Presently her cough ceased and she fell into a profound sleep, which lasted until twelve o'clock the next day. When I returned from shooting, I was informed that she was still asleep and could not be awoke, and I had great difficulty in awaking her. That night there was a large dinner party, and, unluckily, I sat opposite to her. Presently she again became drowsy, and had to be led from the table, alleging, to my confusion, that I was again mesmerizing her. So susceptible did she become to my supposed mesmeric influence, which I vainly assured her, as was the case, that I was very far from exercising or attempting to exercise, that it was found expedient to take her up to London. I was out riding in the afternoon that she left, and as we passed the railway station, my host, who was riding with me, suggested that, as his friends were just leaving by that train, he would like to alight and take leave of them. I dismounted with him and went on to the platform, and avoided any leave-taking; but unfortunately in walking up and down it seems that I twice passed the window of the young lady's carriage. She was again self-mesmerized, and fell into a sleep which lasted throughout the journey, and recurred at intervals for some days afterward."

In commenting on this, Dr. Hart notes that in reality mesmerism is self-produced, and the will of the operator, even when exercised directly against it, has no effect if the subject believes that the will is being operated in favor of it. Says he: "So long as the person operated on believed that my will was that she should sleep, sleep followed. The most energetic willing in my internal consciousness that there should be no sleep, failed to prevent it, where the usual physical methods of hypnotization, stillness, repose, a fixed gaze, or the verbal expression of an order to sleep, were employed."

The dangers of hypnotism have been recognized by the law of every civilized country except the United States, where alone public performances are permitted.

Dr. Cocke says: "I have occasionally seen subjects who complained of headache, vertigo, nausea, and other similar symptoms after having been hypnotized, but these conditions were at a future hypnotic sitting easily remedied by suggestion." Speaking of the use of hypnotism by doctors under conditions of reasonable care, Dr. Cocke says further: "There is one contraindication greater than all the rest. It applies more to the physician than to the patient, more to the masses than to any single individual. It is not confined to hypnotism alone; it has blocked the wheels of human progress through the ages which have gone. It is undue enthusiasm. It is the danger that certain individuals will become so enamored with its charms that other equally valuable means of cure will be ignored. Mental therapeutics has come to stay. It is yet in its infancy and will grow, but, if it were possible to kill it, it would be strangled by the fanaticism and prejudice of its devotees. The whole field is fascinating and alluring. It promises so much that it is in danger of being missed by the ignorant to such an extent that great harm may result. This is true, not only of mental therapeutics and hypnotism, but of every other blessing we possess. Hypnotism has nothing to fear from the senseless skepticism and contempt of those who have no knowledge of the subject." He adds pertinently enough: "While hypnotism can be used in a greater or less degree by every one, it can only be used intelligently by those who understand, not only hypnotism itself, but disease as well."

Dr. Cocke is a firm believer that the right use of hypnotism by intelligent persons does not weaken the will. Says he: "I do not believe there is any danger whatever in this. I have no evidence (and I have studied a large number of hypnotized subjects) that hypnotism will render a subject less capable of exercising his will when he is relieved from the hypnotic trance. I do not believe that it increases in any way his susceptibility to ordinary suggestion."

However, in regard to the dangers of public performances by professional hypnotizers, Dr. Cocke is equally positive. Says he:

"The dangers of public exhibitions, made ludicrous as they are by the operators, should be condemned by all intelligent men and women, not from the danger of hypnotism itself so much as from the liability of the performers to disturb the mental poise of that large mass of ill-balanced individuals which makes up no inconsiderable part of society." In conclusion he says: "Patients have been injured by the misuse of hypnotism. * * * This is true of every remedial agent ever employed for the relief of man. Every article we eat, if wrongly prepared, if stale, or if too much is taken, will be harmful. Every act, every duty of our lives, may, if overdone, become an injury.

"Then, for the sake of clearness, let me state in closing that hypnotism is dangerous only when it is misused, or when it is applied to that large class of persons who are inherently unsound; especially if that mysterious thing we call credulity predominates to a very great extent over the reason and over other faculties of the mind."

CHAPTER IX.

Hypnotism in Medicine.--Anesthesia. --Restoring the Use of Muscles.--Hallucination.--Bad Habits.

Anaesthesia--It is well known that hypnotism may be used to render subjects insensible to pain. Thus numerous startling experiments are performed in public, such as running hatpins through the cheeks or arms, sewing the tongue to the ear, etc. The curious part of it is that the insensibility may be confined to one spot only. Even persons who are not wholly under hypnotic influence may have an arm or a leg, or any smaller part rendered insensible by suggestion, so that no pain will be felt. This has suggested the use of hypnotism in surgery in the place of chloroform, ether, etc.

About the year 1860 some of the medical profession hoped that hypnotism might come into general use for producing insensibility during surgical operations. Dr. Guerineau in Paris reported the following successful operation: The thigh of a patient was amputated. "After the operation," says the doctor, "I spoke to the patient and asked him how he felt. He replied that he felt as if he were in heaven, and he seized hold of my hand and kissed it. Turning to a medical student, he added: 'I was aware of all that was being done to me, and the proof is that I knew my thigh was cut off at the moment when you asked me if I felt any pain.'"

The writer who records this case continues: "This, however, was but a transitory stage. It was soon recognized that a considerable time and a good deal of preparation were necessary to induce the patients to sleep, and medical men had recourse to a more rapid and certain method; that is, chloroform. Thus the year 1860 saw the rise and fall of Braidism as a means of surgical anaesthesia."

One of the most detailed cases of successful use of hypnotism as an anaesthetic was presented to the Hypnotic Congress which met in 1889, by Dr. Fort, professor of anatomy:

"On the 21st of October, 1887, a young Italian tradesman, aged twenty, Jean M--, came to me and asked me to take off a wen he had on his forehead, a little above the right eyebrow. The tumor was about the size of a walnut.

"I was reluctant to make use of chloroform, although the patient wished it, and I tried a short hypnotic experiment. Finding that my patient was easily hypnotizable, I promised to extract the tumor in a painless manner and without the use of chloroform.

"The next day I placed him in a chair and induced sleep, by a fixed gaze, in less than a minute. Two Italian physicians, Drs. Triani and Colombo who were present during the operation, declared that the subject lost all sensibility and that his muscles retained all the different positions in which they were put exactly as in the cataleptic state. The patient saw nothing, felt nothing, and heard nothing, his brain remaining in communication only with me.

"As soon as we had ascertained that the patient was completely under the influence of the hypnotic slumber, I said to him: 'You will sleep for a quarter of an hour,' knowing that the operation would not last longer than that; and he remained seated and perfectly motionless.

"I made a transversal incision two and a half inches long and removed the tumor, which I took out whole. I then pinched the blood vessels with a pair of Dr. Pean's hemostatic pincers, washed the wound and applied a dressing, without making a single ligature. The patient was still sleeping. To maintain the dressing in proper position, I fastened a bandage around his head. While going through the operation I said to the patient, 'Lower your head, raise your head, turn to the right, to the left,' etc., and he obeyed like an automaton. When everything was finished, I said to him, 'Now, wake up.'

"He then awoke, declared that he had felt nothing and did not suffer, and he went away on foot, as if nothing had been done to him.

"Five days after the dressing was removed and the cicatrix was found completely healed."

Hypnotism has been tried extensively for painless dentistry, but with many cases of failure, which got into the courts and thoroughly discredited the attempt except in very special cases.

Restoring the Use of Muscles.--There is no doubt that hypnotism may be extremely useful in curing many disorders that are essentially nervous, especially such cases as those in which a patient has a fixed idea that something is the matter with him when he is not really affected. Cases of that description are often extremely obstinate, and entirely unaffected by the ordinary therapeutic means. Ordinary doctors abandon the cases in despair, but some person who understands "mental suggestion" (for instance, the Christian Science doctors) easily effects a cure. If the regular physician were a student of hypnotism he would know how to manage cases like that.

By way of illustration, we quote reports of two cases, one successful and one unsuccessful. The following is from a report by one of the physicians of the Charity hospital in Paris:

"Gabrielle C------ became a patient of mine toward the end of 1886. She entered the Charity hospital to be under treatment for some accident arising from pulmonary congestion, and while there was suddenly seized with violent attacks of hystero-epilepsy, which first contracted both legs, and finally reduced them to complete immobility.

"She had been in this state of absolute immobility for seven months and I had vainly tried every therapeutic remedy usual in such cases. My intention was first to restore the general constitution of the subject, who was greatly weakened by her protracted stay in bed, and then, at the end of a certain time, to have recourse to hypnotism, and at the opportune moment suggest to her the idea of walking.

"The patient was hypnotized every morning, and the first degree (that of lethargy), then the cataleptic, and finally the somnambulistic states were produced. After a certain period of somnambulism she began to move, and unconsciously took a few steps across the ward. Soon after it was suggested--the locomotor powers having recovered their physical functions--that she should walk when awake. This she was able to do, and in some weeks the cure was complete. In this case, however, we had the ingenious idea of changing her personality at the moment when we induced her to walk. The patient fancied she was somebody else, and as such, and in this roundabout manner, we satisfactorily attained the object proposed."

The following is Professor Delboeuf's account of Dr. Bernheim's mode of suggestion at the hospital at Nancy. A robust old man of about seventy-five years of age, paralyzed by sciatica, which caused him intense pain, was brought in. "He could not put a foot to the ground without screaming with pain. 'Lie down, my poor friend; I will soon relieve you.' Dr. Bernheim says. 'That is impossible, doctor.' 'You will see.' 'Yes, we shall see, but I tell you, we shall see nothing!' On hearing this answer I thought suggestion will be of no use in this case. The old man looked sullen and stubborn. Strangely enough, he soon went off to sleep, fell into a state of catalepsy, and was insensible when pricked. But when Monsieur Bernheim said to him, 'Now you can walk, he replied, 'No, I cannot; you are telling me to do an impossible thing.' Although Monsieur Bernheim failed in this instance, I could not but admire his skill. After using every means of persuasion, insinuation and coaxing, he suddenly took up an imperative tone, and in a sharp, abrupt voice that did not admit a refusal, said: 'I tell you you can walk; get up.' 'Very well,' replied the old follow; 'I must if you insist upon it.' And he got out of bed. No sooner, however, had his foot touched the floor than he screamed even louder than before. Monsieur Bernheim ordered him to step out. 'You tell me to do what is impossible,' he again replied, and he did not move. He had to be allowed to go to bed again, and the whole time the experiment lasted he maintained an obstinate and ill-tempered air."

These two cases give an admirable picture of the cases that can be and those that cannot be cured by hypnotism, or any other method of mental suggestion.

Hallucination.--"Hallucinations," says a medical authority, "are very common among those who are partially insane. They occur as a result of fever and frequently accompany delirium. They result from an impoverished condition of the blood, especially if it is due to starvation, indigestion, and the use of drugs like belladonna, hyoscyarnus, stramonium, opium, chloral, cannabis indica, and many more that might be mentioned."

Large numbers of cases of attempted cure by hypnotism, successful and unsuccessful, might be quoted. There is no doubt that in the lighter forms of partial insanity, hypnotism may help many patients, though not all; but when the disease of the brain has gone farther, especially when a well developed lesion exists in the brain, mental treatment is of little avail, even if it can be practiced at all.

A few general remarks by Dr. Bernheim will be interesting. Says he:

"The mode of suggestion should be varied and adapted to the special suggestibility of the subject. A simple word does not always suffice in impressing the idea upon the mind. It is sometimes necessary to reason, to prove, to convince; in some cases to affirm decidedly, in others to insinuate gently; for in the condition of sleep, just as in the waking condition, the moral individuality of each subject persists according to his character, his inclinations, his impressionability, etc. Hypnosis does not run all subjects into a uniform mold, and make pure and simple automatons out of them, moved solely by the will of the hypnotist; it increases cerebral docility; it makes the automatic activity preponderate over the will. But the latter persists to a certain degree; the subject thinks, reasons, discusses, accepts more readily than in the waking condition, but does not always accept, especially in the light degrees of sleep. In these cases we must know the patient's character, his particular psychical condition, in order to make an impression upon him."

Bad Habits.--The habit of the excessive use of alcoholic drinks, morphine, tobacco, or the like, may often be decidedly helped by hypnotism, if the patient wants to be helped. The method of operation is simple. The operator hypnotizes the subject, and when he is in deep sleep suggests that on awaking he will feel a deep disgust for the article he is in the habit of taking, and if he takes it will be affected by nausea, or other unpleasant symptoms. In most cases the suggested result takes place, provided the subject can be hypnotized at all; but unless the patient is himself anxious to break the habit fixed upon him, the unpleasant effects soon wear off and he is as bad as ever.

Dr. Cocke treated a large number of cases, which he reports in detail in his book on hypnotism. In a fair proportion of the cases he was successful; in some cases completely so. In other cases he failed entirely, owing to lack of moral stamina in the patient himself. His conclusions seem to be that hypnotism may be made a very effective aid to moral suasion, but after all, character is the chief force which throws off such habits once they are fixed. The morphine habit is usually the result of a doctor's prescription at some time, and it is practiced more or less involuntarily. Such cases are often materially helped by the proper suggestions.

The same is true of bad habits in children. The weak may be strengthened by the stronger nature, and hypnotism may come in as an effective aid to moral influence. Here again character is the deciding factor.

Dr. James R. Cocke devotes a considerable part of his book on "Hypnotism" to the use of hypnotism in medical practice, and for further interesting details the reader is referred to that able work.

CHAPTER X.

Hypnotism of Animals.--Snake Charming.

We are all familiar with the snake charmer, and the charming of birds by snakes. How much hypnotism there is in these performances it would be hard to say. It is probable that a bird is fascinated to some extent by the steady gaze of a serpent's eyes, but fear will certainly paralyze a bird as effectively as hypnotism.

Father Kircher was the first to try a familiar experiment with hens and cocks. If you hold a hen's head with the beak upon a piece of board, and then draw a chalk line from the beak to the edge of the board, the hen when released will continue to hold her head in the same position for some time, finally walking slowly away, as if roused from a stupor. Farmers' wives often try a sort of hypnotic experiment on hens they wish to transfer from one nest to another when sitting. They put the hen's head under her wing and gently rock her to and fro till she apparently goes to sleep, when she may be carried to another nest and will remain there afterward.

Horses are frequently managed by a steady gaze into their eyes. Dr. Moll states that a method of hypnotizing horses named after its inventor as Balassiren has been introduced into Austria by law for the shoeing of horses in the army.

We have all heard of the snake charmers of India, who make the snakes imitate all their movements. Some suppose this is by hypnotization. It may be the result of training, however. Certainly real charmers of wild beasts usually end by being bitten or injured in some other way, which would seem to show that the hypnotization does not always work, or else it does not exist at all.

We have some fairly well known instances of hypnotism produced in animals. Lafontaine, the magnetizer, some thirty years ago held public exhibitions in Paris in which he reduced cats, dogs, squirrels and lions to such complete insensibility that they felt neither pricks nor blows.

The Harvys or Psylles of Egypt impart to the ringed snake the appearance of a stick by pressure on the head, which induces a species of tetanus, says E. W. Lane.

The following description of serpent charming by the Aissouans of the province of Sous, Morocco, will be of interest:

"The principal charmer began by whirling with astonishing rapidity in a kind of frenzied dance around the wicker basket that contained the serpents, which were covered by a goatskin. Suddenly he stopped, plunged his naked arm into the basket, and drew out a cobra de capello, or else a haje, a fearful reptile which is able to swell its head by spreading out the scales which cover it, and which is thought to be Cleopatra's asp, the serpent of Egypt. In Morocco it is known as the buska. The charmer folded and unfolded the greenish-black viper, as if it were a piece of muslin; he rolled it like a turban round his head, and continued his dance while the serpent maintained its position, and seemed to follow every movement and wish of the dancer.

"The buska was then placed on the ground, and raising itself straight on end, in the attitude it assumes on desert roads to attract travelers, began to sway from right to left, following the rhythm of the music. The Aissoua, whirling more and more rapidly in constantly narrowing circles, plunged his hand once more into the basket, and pulled out two of the most venomous reptiles of the desert of Sous; serpents thicker than a man's arm, two or three feet long, whose shining scales are spotted black or yellow, and whose bite sends, as it were, a burning fire through the veins. This reptile is probably the torrida dipsas of antiquity. Europeans now call it the leffah.

"The two leffahs, more vigorous and less docile than the buska, lay half curled up, their heads on one side, ready to dart forward, and followed with glittering eyes the movements of the dancer. * * * Hindoo charmers are still more wonderful; they juggle with a dozen different species of reptiles at the same time, making them come and go, leap, dance, and lie down at the sound of the charmer's whistle, like the gentlest of tame animals. These serpents have never been known to bite their charmers."

It is well known that some animals, like the opossum, feign death when caught. Whether this is to be compared to hypnotism is doubtful. Other animals, called hibernating, sleep for months with no other food than their fat, but this, again, can hardly be called hypnotism.

CHAPTER XI.
A Scientific Explanation of Hypnotism.--Dr. Hart's Theory.

In the introduction to this book the reader will find a summary of the theories of hypnotism. There is no doubt that hypnotism is a complex state which cannot be explained in an offhand way in a sentence or two. There are, however, certain aspects of hypnotism which we may suppose sufficiently explained by certain scientific writers on the subject.

First, what is the character of the delusions apparently created in the mind of a person in the hypnotic condition by a simple word of mouth statement, as when a physician says, "Now, I am going to cut your leg off, but it will not hurt you in the least," and the patient suffers nothing?

In answer to this question, Professor William James of Harvard College, one of the leading authorities on the scientific aspects of psychical phenomena in this country, reports the following experiments:

"Make a stroke on a paper or blackboard, and tell the subject it is not there, and he will see nothing but the clean paper or board. Next, he not looking, surround the original stroke with other strokes exactly like it, and ask him what he sees. He will point out one by one the new strokes and omit the original one every time, no matter how numerous the next strokes may be, or in what order they are arranged. Similarly, if the original single line, to which he is blind, be doubled by a prism of sixteen degrees placed before one of his eyes (both being kept open), he will say that he now sees one stroke, and point in the direction in which lies the image seen through the prism.

"Another experiment proves that he must see it in order to ignore it. Make a red cross, invisible to the hypnotic subject, on a sheet of white paper, and yet cause him to look fixedly at a dot on the paper on or near the red cross; he wills on transferring his eye to the blank sheet, see a bluish-green after image of the cross. This proves that it has impressed his sensibility. He has felt but not perceived it. He had actually ignored it; refused to recognize it, as it were."

Dr. Ernest Hart, an English writer, in an article in the British Medical Journal, gives a general explanation of the phenomena of hypnotism which we may accept as true so far as it goes, but which is evidently incomplete. He seems to minimize personal influence too much--that personal influence which we all exert at various times, and which he ignores, not because he would deny it, but because he fears lending countenance to the magnetic fluid and other similar theories. Says he:

"We have arrived at the point at which it will be plain that the condition produced in these cases, and known under a varied jargon invented either to conceal ignorance, to express hypotheses, or to mask the design of impressing the imagination and possibly prey upon the pockets of a credulous and wonder-loving public--such names as mesmeric condition, magnetic sleep, clairvoyance, electro-biology, animal magnetism, faith trance, and many other aliases--such a condition, I say, is always subjective. It is independent of passes or gestures; it has no relation to any fluid emanating from the operator; it has no relation to his will, or to any influence which he exercises upon inanimate objects; distance does not affect it, nor proximity, nor the intervention of any conductors or non-conductors, whether silk or glass or stone, or even a brick wall. We can transmit the order to sleep by telephone or by telegraph. We can practically get the same results while eliminating even the operator, if we can contrive to influence the imagination or to affect the physical condition of the subject by any one of a great number of contrivances.

"What does all this mean? I will refer to one or two facts in relation to the structure and function of the brain, and show one or two simple experiments of very ancient parentage and date, which will, I think, help to an explanation. First, let us recall something of what we know of the anatomy and localization of function in the brain, and of the nature of ordinary sleep. The brain, as you know, is a complicated organ, made up internally of nerve masses, or ganglia, of which the central and underlying masses are connected with the automatic functions and involuntary actions of the body (such as the action of the heart, lungs, stomach, bowels, etc.), while the investing surface shows a system of complicated convolutions rich in gray matter, thickly sown with microscopic cells, in which the nerve ends terminate. At the base of the brain is a complete circle of arteries, from which spring great numbers of small arterial vessels, carrying a profuse blood supply throughout the whole mass, and capable of contraction in small tracts, so that small areas of the brain may, at any given moment, become bloodless, while other parts of the brain may simultaneously become highly congested. Now, if the brain or any part of it be deprived of the circulation of blood through it, or be rendered partially bloodless, or if it be excessively congested and overloaded with blood, or if it be subjected to local pressure, the part of the brain so acted upon ceases to be capable of exercising its functions. The regularity of the action of the brain and the sanity and completeness of the thought which is one of the functions of its activity depend upon the healthy regularity of the quantity of blood passing through all its parts, and upon the healthy quality of the blood so circulating. If we press upon the carotid arteries which pass up through the neck to form the arterial circle of Willis, at the base of the brain, within the skull--of which I have already spoken, and which supplies the brain with blood--we quickly, as every one knows, produce insensibility. Thought is abolished, consciousness lost. And if we continue the pressure, all those automatic actions of the body, such as the beating of the heart, the breathing motions of the lungs, which maintain life and are controlled by the lower brain centers of ganglia, are quickly stopped and death ensues.

"We know by observation in cases where portions of the skull have been removed, either in men or in animals, that during natural sleep the upper part of the brain--its convoluted surface, which in health and in the waking state is faintly pink, like a blushing cheek, from the color of the blood circulating through the network of capillary arteries--becomes white and almost bloodless. It is in these upper convolutions of the brain, as we also know, that the will and the directing power are resident; so that in sleep the will is abolished and consciousness fades gradually away, as the blood is pressed out by the contraction of the arteries. So, also, the consciousness and the directing will may be abolished by altering the quality of the blood passing through the convolutions of the brain. We may introduce a volatile substance, such as chloroform, and its first effect will be to abolish consciousness and induce profound slumber and a blessed insensibility to pain. The like effects will follow more slowly upon the absorption of a drug, such as opium; or we may induce hallucinations by introducing into the blood other toxic substances, such as Indian hemp or stramonium. We are not conscious of the mechanism producing the arterial contraction and the bloodlessness of those convolutions related to natural sleep. But we are not altogether without control over them. We can, we know, help to compose ourselves to sleep, as we say in ordinary language. We retire into a darkened room, we relieve ourselves from the stimulus of the special senses, we free ourselves from the influence of noises, of strong light, of powerful colors, or of tactile impressions. We lie down and endeavor to soothe brain activity by driving away disturbing thoughts, or, as people sometimes say, 'try to think of nothing.' And, happily, we generally succeed more or less well. Some people possess an even more marked control over this mechanism of sleep. I can generally succeed in putting myself to sleep at any hour of the day, either in the library chair or in the brougham. This is, so to speak, a process of self-hypnotization, and I have often practiced it when going from house to house, when in the midst of a busy practice, and I sometimes have amused my friends and family by exercising this faculty, which I do not think it very difficult to acquire. (We also know that many persons can wake at a fixed hour in the morning by setting their minds upon it just before going to sleep.) Now, there is something here which deserves a little further examination, but which it would take too much time to develop fully at present. Most people know something of what is meant by reflex action. The nerves which pass from the various organs to the brain convey with, great rapidity messages to its various parts, which are answered by reflected waves of impulse. If the soles of the feet be tickled, contraction of the toes, or involuntary laughter, will be excited, or perhaps only a shuddering and skin contraction, known as goose-skin. The irritation of the nerve-end in the skin has carried a message to the involuntary or voluntary ganglia of the brain which has responded by reflecting back again nerve impulses which have contracted the muscles of the feet or skin muscles, or have given rise to associated ideas and explosion of laughter. In the same way, if during sleep heat be applied to the soles of the feet, dreams of walking over hot surfaces--Vesuvius or Fusiyama, or still hotter places--may be produced, or dreams of adventure on frozen surfaces or in arctic regions may be created by applying ice to the feet of the sleeper.

"Here, then, it is seen that we have a mechanism in the body, known to physiologists as the ideo-motor, or sensory motor system of nerves, which can produce, without the consciousness of the individual and automatically, a series of muscular contractions. And remember that the coats of the arteries are muscular and contractile under the influence of external stimuli, acting without the help of the consciousness, or when the consciousness is in abeyance. I will give another example of this, which completes the chain of phenomena in the natural brain and the natural body I wish to bring under notice in explanation of the true as distinguished from the false, or falsely interpreted, phenomena of hypnotism, mesmerism and electro-biology. I will take the excellent illustration quoted by Dr. B. W. Carpenter in his old-time, but valuable, book on 'The Physiology of the Brain.' When a hungry man sees food, or when, let us say, a hungry boy looks into a cookshop, he becomes aware of a watering of the mouth and a gnawing sensation at the stomach. What does this mean? It means that the mental impression made upon him by the welcome and appetizing spectacle has caused a secretion of saliva and of gastric juice; that is to say, the brain has, through the ideo-motor set of nerves, sent a message which has dilated the vessels around the salivary and gastric glands, increased the flow of blood through them and quickened their secretion. Here we have, then, a purely subjective mental activity acting through a mechanism of which the boy is quite ignorant, and which he is unable to control, and producing that action on the vessels of dilation or contraction which, as we have seen, is the essential condition of brain activity and the evolution of thought, and is related to the quickening or the abolition of consciousness, and to the activity or abeyance of function in the will centers and upper convolutions of the brain, as in its other centers of localization.

"Here, then, we have something like a clue to the phenomena--phenomena which, as I have pointed out, are similar to and have much in common with mesmeric sleep, hypnotism or electro-biology. We have already, I hope, succeeded in eliminating from our minds the false theory--the theory, that is to say, experimentally proved to be false--that the will, or the gestures, or the magnetic or vital fluid of the operator are necessary for the abolition of the consciousness and the abeyance of the will of the subject. We now see that ideas arising in the mind of the subject are sufficient to influence the circulation in the brain of the person operated on, and such variations of the blood supply of the brain as are adequate to produce sleep in the natural state, or artificial slumber, either by total deprivation or by excessive increase or local aberration in the quantity or quality of blood. In a like manner it is possible to produce coma and prolonged insensibility by pressure of the thumbs on the carotid; or hallucination, dreams and visions by drugs, or by external stimulation of the nerves. Here again the consciousness may be only partially affected, and the person in whom sleep, coma or hallucination is produced, whether by physical means or by the influence of suggestion, may remain subject to the will of others and incapable of exercising his own volition."

In short, Dr. Hart's theory is that hypnotism comes from controlling the blood supply of the brain, cutting off the supply from parts or increasing it in other parts. This theory is borne out by the well-known fact that some persons can blush or turn pale at will; that some people always blush on the mention of certain things, or calling up certain ideas. Certain other ideas will make them turn pale. Now, if certain parts of the brain are made to blush or turn pale, there is no doubt that hypnotism will follow, since blushing and turning pale are known to be due to the opening and closing of the blood-vessels. We may say that the subject is induced by some means to shut the blood out of certain portions of the brain, and keep it out until he is told to let it in again.

CHAPTER XII.
Telepathy and Clairvoyance.--Peculiar Power in Hypnotic State.--Experiments.--"Phantasms of the Living" Explained by Telepathy

It has already been noticed that persons in the hypnotic state seem to have certain of their senses greatly heightened in power. They can remember, see and hear things that ordinary persons would be entirely ignorant of. There is abundant evidence that a supersensory perception is also developed, entirely beyond the most highly developed condition of the ordinary senses, such as being able to tell clearly what some other person is doing at a great distance. In view of the discovery of the X or Roentgen ray, the ability to see through a stone wall does not seem so strange as it did before that discovery.

It is on power of supersensory, or extra-sensory perception that what is known as telepathy and clairvoyance are based. That such things really exist, and are not wholly a matter of superstition has been thoroughly demonstrated in a scientific way by the British Society for Psychical Research, and kindred societies in various parts of the world. Strictly speaking, such phenomena as these are not a part of hypnotism, but our study of hypnotism will enable us to understand them to some extent, and the investigation of them is a natural corollary to the study of hypnotism, for the reason that it has been found that these extraordinary powers are often possessed by persons under hypnotic influence. Until the discovery of hypnotism there was little to go on in conducting a scientific investigation, because clairvoyance could not be produced by any artificial means, and so could not be studied under proper restrictive conditions.

We will first quote two experiments performed by Dr. Cocke which the writer heard him describe with his own lips.

The first case was that of a girl suffering from hysterical tremor. The doctor had hypnotized her for the cure of it, and accidentally stumbled on an example of thought transference. She complained on one occasion of a taste of spice in her mouth. As the doctor had been chewing some spice, he at once guessed that this might be telepathy. Nothing was said at the time, but the next time the girl was hypnotized, the doctor put a quinine tablet in his mouth. The girl at once asked for water, and said she had a very bitter taste in her mouth. The water was given her, and the doctor went behind a screen, where he put cayenne pepper in his mouth, severely burning himself. No one but the doctor knew of the experiment at the time. The girl immediately cried and became so hysterical that she had to be awakened. The burning in her mouth disappeared as soon as she came out of the hypnotic state, but the doctor continued to suffer. Nearly three hundred similar experiments with thirty-six different subjects were tried by Dr. Cocke, and of these sixty-nine were entirely successful. The others were doubtful or complete failures.

The most remarkable of the experiments may be given in the doctor's own words: "I told the subject to remain perfectly still for five minutes and to relate to me at the end of this time any sensation he might experience. I passed into another room and closed the door and locked it; went into a closet in the room and closed the door after me; took down from the shelf, first a linen sheet, then a pasteboard box, then a toy engine, owned by a child in the house. I went back to my subject and asked him what experience he had had.

"He said I seemed to go into another room, and from thence into a dark closet. I wanted something off the shelf, but did not know what. I took down from the shelf a piece of smooth cloth, a long, square pasteboard box and a tin engine. These were all the sensations he had experienced. I asked him if he saw the articles with his eyes which I had removed from the shelf. He answered that the closet was dark and that he only felt them with his hands. I asked him how he knew that the engine was tin. He said: 'By the sound of it.' As my hands touched it I heard the wheels rattle. Now the only sound made by me while in the closet was simply the rattling of the wheels of the toy as I took it off the shelf. This could not possibly have been heard, as the subject was distant from me two large rooms, and there were two closed doors between us, and the noise was very slight. Neither could the subject have judged where I went, as I had on light slippers which made no noise. The subject had never visited the house before, and naturally did not know the contents of the closet as he was carefully observed from the moment he entered the house."

Many similar experiments are on record. Persons in the hypnotic condition have been able to tell what other persons were doing in distant parts of a city; could tell the pages of the books they might be reading and the numbers of all sorts of articles. While in London the writer had an opportunity of witnessing a performance of this kind. There was a young boy who seemed to have this peculiar power. A queer old desk had come into the house from Italy, and as it was a valuable piece of furniture, the owner was anxious to learn its pedigree. Without having examined the desk beforehand in any way the boy, during one of his trances, said that in a certain place a secret spring would be found which would open an unknown drawer, and behind that drawer would be found the name of the maker of the desk and the date 1639. The desk was at once examined, and the name and date found exactly as described. It is clear in this case that this information could not have been in the mind of any one, unless it were some person in Italy, whence the desk had come. It is more likely that the remarkable supersensory power given enabled reading through the wood.

We may now turn our attention to another class of phenomena of great interest, and that is the visions persons in the ordinary state have of friends who are on the point of death. It would seem that by an extraordinary effort the mind of a person in the waking state might be impressed through a great distance. At the moment of death an almost superhuman mental effort is more likely and possible than at any other time, and it is peculiar that these visions or phantasms are largely confined to that moment. The natural explanation that rises to the ordinary mind is, of course, "Spirits." This supposition is strengthened by the fact that the visions sometimes appear immediately after death, as well as at the time and just before. This may be explained, however, on the theory that the ordinary mind is not easily impressed, and when unconsciously impressed some time may elapse before the impression becomes perceptible to the conscious mind, just as in passing by on a swift train, we may see something, but not realize that we have seen it till some time afterward, when we remember what we have unconsciously observed.

The British Society for Psychical Research has compiled two large volumes of carefully authenticated cases, which are published under the title, "Phantasms of the Living." We quote one or two interesting cases.

A Miss L. sends the following report: January 4, 1886.

"On one of the last days of July, about the year 1860, at 3 o'clock p.m. , I was sitting in the drawing room at the Rectory, reading, and my thoughts entirely occupied. I suddenly looked up and saw most distinctly a tall, thin old gentleman enter the room and walk to the table. He wore a peculiar, old-fashioned cloak which I recognized as belonging to my great-uncle. I then looked at him closely and remembered his features and appearance perfectly, although I had not seen him since I was quite a child. In his hand was a roll of paper, and he appeared to be very agitated. I was not in the least alarmed, as I firmly believed he was my uncle, not knowing then of his illness. I asked him if he wanted my father, who, as I said, was not at home. He then appeared still more agitated and distressed, but made no remark. He then left the room, passing through the open door. I noticed that, although it was a very wet day, there was no appearance of his having walked either in mud or rain. He had no umbrella, but a thick walking stick, which I recognized at once when my father brought it home after the funeral. On questioning the servants, they declared that no one had rung the bell; neither did they see any one enter. My father had a letter by the next post, asking him to go at once to my uncle, who was very ill in Leicestershire. He started at once, but on his arrival was told that his uncle had died at exactly 3 o'clock that afternoon, and had asked for him by name several times in an anxious and troubled manner, and a roll of paper was found under his pillow.

"I may mention that my father was his only nephew, and, having no son, he always led him to think that he would have a considerable legacy. Such, however, was not the case, and it is supposed that, as they were always good friends, he was influenced in his last illness, and probably, when too late, he wished to alter his will."

In answer to inquiries, Miss L. adds:

"I told my mother and an uncle at once about the strange appearance before the news arrived, and also my father directly he returned, all of whom are now dead. They advised me to dismiss it from my memory, but agreed that it could not be imagination, as I described my uncle so exactly, and they did not consider me to be either of a nervous or superstitious temperament.

"I am quite sure that I have stated the facts truthfully and correctly. The facts are as fresh in my memory as if they happened only yesterday, although so many years have passed away.

"I can assure you that nothing of the sort ever occurred before or since. Neither have I been subject to nervous or imaginative fancies. This strange apparition was in broad daylight, and as I was only reading the 'Illustrated Newspaper,' there was nothing to excite my imagination."

Hundreds of cases of this kind have been reported by persons whose truthfulness cannot be doubted, and every effort has been made to eliminate possibility of hallucination or accidental fancy. That things of this kind do occur may be said to be scientifically proven.

Such facts as these have stimulated experiment in the direction of testing thought transference. These experiments have usually been in the reading of numbers and names, and a certain measure of success has resulted. It may be added, however, that no claimants ever appeared for various banknotes deposited in strong-boxes, to be turned over to any one who would read the numbers. Just why success was never attained under these conditions it would be hard to say. The writer once made a slight observation in this direction. When matching pennies with his brother he found that if the other looked at the penny he could match it nearly every time. There may have been some unconscious expression of face that gave the clue. Persons in hypnotic trance are expert muscle readers. For instance, let such a person take your hand and then go through the alphabet, naming the letters. If you have any word in your mind, as the muscle reader comes to each letter the muscles will unconsciously contract. By giving attention h the muscles you can make them contract on the wrong letters and entirely mislead such a person.

CHAPTER XIII.

The Confessions of Medium.--Spiritualistic Phenomena Explained on Theory of Telepathy.--Interesting Statement of Mrs. Piper, the Famous Medium of the Psychical Research Society.

The subject of spiritualism has been very thoroughly investigated by the Society for Psychical Research, both in England and this country, and under circumstances so peculiarly advantageous that a world of light has been thrown on the connection between hypnotism and this strange phenomenon.

Professor William James, the professor of psychology at Harvard University, was fortunate enough some years ago to find a perfect medium who was not a professional and whose character was such as to preclude fraud. This was Mrs. Leonora E. Piper, of Boston. For many years she remained in the special employ of the Society for Psychical Research, and the members of that society were able to study her case under every possible condition through a long period of time. Not long ago she resolved to give up her engagement, and made a public statement over her own signature which is full of interest.

A brief history of her life and experiences will go far toward furnishing the general reader a fair explanation of clairvoyant and spiritualistic phenomena.

Mrs. Piper was the wife of a modest tailor, and lived on Pinckney street, back of Beacon Hill. She was married in 1881, and it was not until May 16, 1884, that her first child was born. A little more than a month later, on June 29, she had her first trance experience. Says she: "I remember the date distinctly, because it was two days after my first birthday following the birth of my first child." She had gone to Dr. J. R. Cocke, the great authority on hypnotism and a practicing physician of high scientific attainments. "During the interview," says Mrs. Piper, "I was partly unconscious for a few minutes. On the following Sunday I went into a trance."

She appears to have slipped into it unconsciously. She surprised her friends by saying some very odd things, none of which she remembered when she came to herself. Not long after she did it again. A neighbor, the wife of a merchant, when she heard the things that had been said, assured Mrs. Piper that it must be messages from the spirit world. The atmosphere in Boston was full of talk of that kind, and it was not hard for people to believe that a real medium of spirit communication had been found. The merchant's wife wanted a sitting, and Mrs. Piper arranged one, for which she received her first dollar.

She had discovered that she could go into trances by an effort of her own will. She would sit down at a table, with her sitter opposite, and leaning her head on a pillow, go off into the trance after a few minutes of silence. There was a clock behind her. She gave her sitters an hour, sometimes two hours, and they wondered how she knew when the hour had expired. At any rate, when the time came around she awoke. In describing her experiences she has said:

"At first when I sat in my chair and leaned my head back and went into the trance state, the action was attended by something of a struggle. I always felt as if I were undergoing an anesthetic, but of late years I have slipped easily into the condition, leaning the head forward. On coming out of it I felt stupid and dazed. At first I said disconnected things. It was all a gibberish, nothing but gibberish. Then I began to speak some broken French phrases. I had studied French two years, but did not speak it well."

Once she had an Italian for sitter, who could speak no English and asked questions in Italian. Mrs. Piper could speak no Italian, indeed did not understand a word of it, except in her trance state. But she had no trouble in understanding her sitter.

After a while her automatic utterance announced the personality of a certain Dr. Phinuit, who was said to have been a noted French physician who had died long before. His "spirit" controlled her for a number of years. After some time Dr. Phinuit was succeeded by one "Pelham," and finally by "Imperator" and "Rector."

As the birth of her second child approached Mrs. Piper gave up what she considered a form of hysteria; but after the birth of the child the sittings, paid for at a dollar each, began again. Dr. Hodgson, of the London Society for Psychical Research, saw her at the house of Professor James, and he became so interested in her case that he decided to take her to London to be studied. She spent nearly a year abroad; and after her return the American branch of the Society for Psychical Research was formed, and for a long time Mrs. Piper received a salary to sit exclusively for the society. Their records and reports are full of the things she said and did.

Every one who investigated Mrs. Piper had to admit that her case was full of mystery. But if one reads the reports through from beginning to end one cannot help feeling that her spirit messages are filled with nonsense, at least of triviality. Here is a specimen--and a fair specimen, too--of the kind of communication Pelham gave. He wrote out the message. It referred to a certain famous man known in the reports as Mr. Marte. Pelham is reported to have written by Mrs. Piper's hand:

"That he (Mr. Marte), with his keen brain and marvelous perception, will be interested, I know. He was a very dear friend of X. I was exceedingly fond of him. Comical weather interests both he and I--me--him--I know it all. Don't you see I correct these? Well, I am not less intelligent now. But there are many difficulties. I am far clearer on all points than I was shut up in the prisoned body (prisoned, prisoning or imprisoned you ought to say). No, I don't mean, to get it that way. 'See here, H, don't view me with a critic's eye, but pass my imperfections by.' Of course, I know all that as well as anybody on your sphere (of course). Well, I think so. I tell you, old fellow, it don't do to pick all these little errors too much when they amount to nothing in one way. You have light enough and brain enough, I know, to understand my explanations of being shut up in this body, dreaming, as it were, and trying to help on science."

Some people would say that Pelham had had a little too much whisky toddy when he wrote that rambling, meaningless string of words. Or we can suppose that Mrs. Piper was dreaming. We see in the last sentence a curious mixture of ideas that must have been in her mind. She herself says:

"I do not see how anybody can look on all that as testimony from another world. I cannot see but that it must have been an unconscious expression of my subliminal self, writing such stuff as dreams are made of."

In another place Mrs. Piper makes the following direct statement: "I never heard of anything being said by myself while in a trance state which might not have been latent in:

"1. My own mind.

"2. In the mind of the person in charge of the sitting.

"3. In the mind of the person who was trying to get communication with some one in another state of existence, or some companion present with such person, or,

"4. In the mind of some absent person alive somewhere else in the world."

Writing in the Psychological Review in 1898, Professor James says:

"Mrs. Piper's trance memory is no ordinary human memory, and we have to explain its singular perfection either as the natural endowment of her solitary subliminal self, or as a collection of distinct memory systems, each with a communicating spirit as its vehicle.

"The spirit hypothesis exhibits a vacancy, triviality, and incoherence of mind painful to think of as the state of the departed, and coupled with a pretension to impress one, a disposition to 'fish' and face around and disguise the essential hollowness which is, if anything, more painful still. Mr. Hodgson has to resort to the theory that, although the communicants probably are spirits, they are in a semi-comatose or sleeping state while communicating, and only half aware of what is going on, while the habits of Mrs. Piper's neural organism largely supply the definite form of words, etc., in which the phenomenon is clothed."

After considering other theories Professor James concludes:

"The world is evidently more complex than we are accustomed to think it, the absolute 'world ground' in particular being farther off than we are wont to think it."

Mrs. Piper is reported to have said:

"Of what occurs after I enter the trance period I remember nothing-- nothing of what I said or what was said to me. I am but a passive agent in the hands of powers that control me. I can give no account of what becomes of me during a trance. The wisdom and inspired eloquence which of late has been conveyed to Dr. Hodgson through my mediumship is entirely beyond my understanding. I do not pretend to understand it, and can give no explanation-- I simply know that I have the power of going into a trance when I wish."

Professor James says: "The Piper phenomena are the most absolutely baffling thing I know."

Professor Hudson, Ph.D., LL.D., author of "The Law of Psychic Phenomena," comes as near giving an explanation of "spiritualism," so called, as any one. He begins by saying:

"All things considered, Mrs. Piper is probably the best 'psychic' now before the public for the scientific investigation of spiritualism and it must be admitted that if her alleged communications from discarnate spirits cannot be traced to any other source, the claims of spiritism have been confirmed."

Then he goes on:

"A few words, however, will make it clear to the scientific mind that her phenomena can be easily accounted for on purely psychological principles, thus:

"Man is endowed with a dual mind, or two minds, or states of consciousness, designated, respectively, as the objective and the subjective. The objective mind is normally unconscious of the content of the subjective mind. The latter is constantly amenable to control by suggestion, and it is exclusively endowed with the faculty of telepathy.

"An entranced psychic is dominated exclusively by her subjective mind, and reason is in abeyance. Hence she is controlled by suggestion, and, consequently, is compelled to believe herself to be a spirit, good or bad, if that suggestion is in any way imparted to her, and she automatically acts accordingly.

"She is in no sense responsible for the vagaries of a Phinuit, for that eccentric personality is the creation of suggestion. But she is also in the condition which enables her to read the subjective minds of others. Hence her supernormal knowledge of the affairs of her sitters. What he knows, or has ever known, consciously or unconsciously (subjective memory being perfect), is easily within her reach.

"Thus far no intelligent psychical researcher will gainsay what I have said. But it sometimes happens that the psychic obtains information that neither she nor the sitter could ever have consciously possessed. Does it necessarily follow that discarnate spirits gave her the information? Spiritists say 'yes,' for this is the 'last ditch' of spiritism.

"Psychologists declare that the telepathic explanation is as valid in the latter class of cases as it obviously is in the former. Thus, telepathy being a power of the subjective mind, messages may be conveyed from one to another at any time, neither of the parties being objectively conscious of the fact. It follows that a telepathist at any following seance with the recipient can reach the content of that message.

"If this argument is valid--and its validity is self-evident--it is impossible to imagine a case that may not be thus explained on psychological principles."

Professor Hudson's argument will appeal to the ordinary reader as good. It may be simplified, however, thus:

We may suppose that Mrs. Piper voluntarily hypnotizes herself. Perhaps she simply puts her conscious reason to sleep. In that condition the rest of her mind is in an exalted state, and capable of telepathy and mind-reading, either of those near at hand or at a distance. Her reason being asleep, she simply dreams, and the questions of her sitter are made to fit into her dream.

If we regard mediums as persons who have the power of hypnotizing themselves and then of doing what we know persons who have been hypnotized by others sometimes do, we have an explanation that covers the whole case perfectly. At the same time, as Professor James warns us, we must believe that the mind is far more complex than we are accustomed to think it.

***